Special Operations

To Eleanor,
a wonderful wife and mother,
and
Catherine,
a finer daughter could not be wanted.

About the author

Timothy John Mullin comes from Scottish-Irish stock and traces his family's arrival in America back to 1690. He views individual firearms ownership as a critical component of liberty and democracy, a view which his ancestors would no doubt have held also.

He was a member of Phi Beta Kappa at St Louis University and graduated *magna cum laude*. He received his *juris doctor* degree from the University of Chicago Law School.

Mullin served seven years in the US Army, first as an infantry officer and later with the Judge Advocate General's Corps, assigned to the Criminal Investigation Division. He was awarded a Meritorious Service Medal upon leaving the military with the rank of captain.

During 1976 and 1977, he served as chief of police for the St Louis Area Support Center and as a deputy US marshal. Since that time, he has served as training officer with local law-enforcement agencies, establishing a modern firearms training program that emphasizes legal and tactical aspects.

Mullin has written numerous articles for a variety of firearms periodicals and law journals and is a frequent speaker on such topics. His books include *Testing the War Weapons – Rifles and Light Machine Guns from Around the World; The Fighting Submachine Gun, Machine Pistol, and Shotgun; Handbook for Handguns; The 100 Greatest Combat Pistols* and *Training the Gunfighter*.

Mullin is married, and his wife, Eleanor, works with him in his St Louis law office. They have one daughter, Catherine, aged 18.

Special Operations
Weapons & Tactics

by T. J. Mullin

Greenhill Books, London

Stackpole Books, Pennsylvania

Greenhill Books

This edition of *Special Operations – weapons & tactics*
first published 2003 by
Greenhill Books, Lional Leventhal Limited,
Park House, 1 Russell Gardens,
London NW11 9NN
www.greenhill books.com
and
Stackpole Books, 5067 Ritter Road,
Mechanicsburg, PA 17055, USA

British Library Cataloguing in Publication data
Mullin, Timothy, J.
Special operations: weapons and tactics
1. Special operations (Military science)
2. Special forces (Military science) - Equipment and supplies
I. Title
355.3'1

Library of Congress Cataloging-in-Publication data available

ISBN 1-85367-527-X

Typeset by Palindrome
Printed in China by Midas Printing International Limited on behalf of
Compass Press Ltd

Contents

Foreword

I believe two anecdotes illustrate the importance of Special Operations soldiers and their weapons in the world of high-tech warfare quite well. The first is an incident from the film *Starship Troopers*, which portrayed the training and combat of infantrymen in a future war. During their basic training, one of the mobile infantrymen asked the drill instructor why it was necessary to learn close combat and throwing techniques with the knife when they would be facing enemies who could destroy a planet by pressing a button. The drill instructor then threw his knife pinning the trainee's hand to a wall and remarked, "You can't push a button now, can you?"

The second occurred when I was commanding a small Special Operations unit in South-East Asia during the Vietnam War. We were assigned to a base which housed the most sophisticated electronic warfare facility in South-East Asia staffed by myriad military and civilian technicians with far higher security clearances than mine. An especially paranoid supervisor at the installation used to enjoy including a visit to my troops as part of his orientation for new EW (electronic warfare) specialists. We would demonstrate how we set ambushes around the base, silent killing techniques with bare hands and blade, use of suppressed weapons and rapid target engagement with CAR-15, M-16 and shotgun. As the supervisor led the new arrivals away, he would chuckle and comment, "If you decide to cross the Mekong and defect to the Communists, these are the guys who will come after you!" I think he intended an entertaining demonstration to make the personnel feel safe within the base's security perimeter, and I think he intended an object lesson for personnel who knew lots of sensitive information!

I guess my point is that the more technological warfare becomes, the more important small groups of highly motivated, highly trained soldiers are, who can infiltrate behind enemy lines or into terrorist camps and quickly deliver a silent "kill" or call in a massive air-strike against the button-pushers or the techies. Many Spec Ops missions require the operators to infiltrate and gather intelligence, then exfiltrate without ever being discovered. Whatever the mission, special operators normally operate in very small groups – four is, in fact, quite a common number for a team. As a result, the artillery support, armor or air power normally available to conventional infantry may not be available to them. Yes, special operators may call in air-strikes or artillery fire, but this is not always an option. In most cases, their first weapon is stealth backed up by their personal small arms and a high degree of weapons training. Even the amount of ammunition carried by the Special Operator may be less than with conventional infantryman since the Spec Ops soldier may have to carry sophisticated communications equipment as well as all the food and water needed for the operation while retaining the ability to cover ground quickly. The Special Operator faces a dilemma: needing enough firepower to lay down a curtain of lead to give devastating covering fire during an escape and evasion scenario, yet not so much that his ability to move fast is impeded. As a result, the Special Operator gives great consideration to the choice of weapons which best suit his mission.

To fit the mission, Special Operations troops may either employ weapons outside the normal military arsenal or employ variations of those weapons designed to enhance their ability to fight and survive. For example, while the current heavy-barreled version of the M-16 rifle may offer greater accuracy at longer range for "leg" infantry, the M-4 carbine is handier for the Special Operator.

The use of specialized weapons may be most noticeable in the pistol-caliber handgun and submachinegun (SMG). While conventional troops generally view the handgun as the weapon for service troops or as a symbol of authority for officers, many Special Operations troops find the pistol an important weapon. Compact enough to be carried concealed when assigned clandestine missions or detailed for VIP protection duties, the pistol may also be carried as a reserve weapon in case of problems with the primary rifle, carbine or submachinegun. The pistol may also be particularly useful in operations in contained environments such as caves, sewers, aircraft, ships, trains or buses. For the Special Operator assigned to counterterrorist operations, skill with the pistol is important for carrying out surgical hostage rescues. The pistol also allows an engagement capability while rappelling, opening doors or performing other functions which leave only one hand free. The pistol is also quite useful as a close-quarter night-fighting weapon when equipped with white-light, laser or infrared illuminator. Finally, the suppressed pistol is not only useful for eliminating sentries, guard dogs or lights, but also allows the Special Operator to fire from within a vehicle without losing aural acuity or to fire within a dangerous environment, such as a clandestine chemical laboratory, when a "wet" suppressor is used.

The SMG extends the advantages of the pistol by offering a more stable shooting platform which maximizes the performance of pistol-caliber ammunition and places multiple hits on a target very quickly. Particularly well-suited to raids against terrorists or enemy command posts on prisoner snatches, the SMG allows rapid target elimination with less possibility of over penetration, a factor which also makes the SMG highly viable for aircraft, train or ship assaults.

Some Special Operators prefer to combine the advantages of the SMG and the carbine and use an SMG-sized weapon chambered for the rifle cartridge. The Russian AKSU, a favorite of the Spetsnaz, is a good example. The US M4 carbine is also widely used as a compromise between SMG and carbine.

The shotgun may also be a key weapon in the Special Operator's battery. For the counterterrorist commando, the shotgun may be used to blow locks or hinges off of a door, while for the member of the US Navy SEALs, the shotgun loaded with special quadrangle buckshot is used to destroy enemy electronics equipment during raids. Still other Special Operators on counterinsurgency operations like the shotgun when walking point (first man on the patrol) for its ability to sweep a trail clean.

Carbines, rifles, light machineguns, knives, hatchets, entrenching tools, machetes, tomahawks, grenades, boots and thumbs – all are weapons which may be used by the Special Operator. It is not by accident that so many Special Operations insignia feature weapons. The Combined Operations patch of World War II prominently displayed the Thompson SMG; the East German parachute qualification badge featured crossed AK 47s; the SAS cap badge bears a winged dagger (actually originally winged Excalibur); and Turkish

Commandos have worn a badge with a grenade emblazoned upon it. These are just a few of the Special Ops insignia which emphasize weapons, but I think the point should be obvious. Special Operations forces engage the enemy in a very close, personal manner. As a result, their training with and choice of small arms is very important.

In this work T J Mullin, who has experience as a Ranger-trained US Army infantry officer and also as a Deputy US Marshal, covers the spectrum of military and police Special Operations weapons. Unlike most previous books of this type, he does not just include the hackneyed photo of the weapon along with a few statistics and a paraphrase of the catalog information. Mullin has fired virtually every weapon discussed in this book and has trained military or police personnel with many of them. He views the weapons as the extensions of the Special Operator and takes a hard look at which ones perform that function best and why.

Whether the reader has served in a Spec Ops unit and filters Mullin's evaluations through his own experience or has never donned a parachute or used a closed-circuit scuba tank but wants to know how the special weapons used by the Special Operators perform, he or she will find this book an informative and fascinating reading experience.

Leroy Thompson
St Louis, Missouri
December, 2001

Introduction

As work on this book wais being finished, Special Operations were (and still are) being covered daily in the press and on television news shows. People who have never before heard of Special Operations all of a sudden are talking about them. Careless references to "American Commando Forces" are bandied about by people who obviously are ignorant of any of the history of this field. Former Special Operators are appearing on cable news shows for 10 to 15 seconds at a time to try to explain what is happening and how their old units will help solve the problem of "world terrorism." I suppose for an author preparing a book he hopes will prove popular, a better time for release could not be imagined.

On the other hand, it is troubling to see all these comments made by "instant experts" in the field and thus feel that you have to attempt to correct all of their factual and philosophical errors which daily mount up.

I have been interested in this area of Special Operations since I was perhaps 12 years old – first from a military standpoint and later, after leaving military service, from a police standpoint. In one way or another I have been testing weapons and training methods that deal with Special Operations for 40 years or more now. During this time, I have read widely on the subject, sought out those who conducted training of famous units and actually carried out Special Operations at both the military and civilian level. By virtue of these acquaintances – friendships in some cases – I have been able to learn a great deal about Special Operations, especially about firearms and training as to what works and what does not work. I have also conducted quite a bit of training over the years with units that vary widely in both skill level as well as mission requirements, so I believe I understand the concerns of those who are charged with leading such units, having been in that position myself, as well as those who are the trainers.

Hopefully what follows, representing a lot of what I have learned over the years, will prove helpful to you, the reader, if you are a member of a Special Operations unit or alternatively a trainer of such a unit. If you are neither, then if only a serious student of the field, you will learn a few things or at least get some mental stimulation from my comments which reflect my experiences and may be different than yours. I recognize that much of my experience has been with US-based agencies, but I have studied and been with British and French units and trained with former Rhodesian / South African operatives so I do not think I am too parochial. Opinions and experiences differ, but I myself find any position that is based on solid logic and real-world experience is useful to consider and ponder. I also believe that any book or article that has at least one good idea is a work worth buying and reading. Hopefully you will find at least one item here that will merit the expenditure of your fortune and time.

I would like to thank here those who have helped contribute to making this work possible. My secretary, Debbie Gallop, who has learned much more than she ever wanted to know about guns, is, I am certain, now at the same stage about Special Operations. Her diligence and hard work have been, as always, a great assistance to me. I also wish to thank my friends who have helped me evaluate and experiment with my theories over the years in this field. Leroy Thompson, who was a well-known Special Operations operative in his earlier years and is a trainer now, has been of great assistance over the last 20 or so years we have been shooting together. My friend, Chief Edward Seyffert, has always been more than willing to try out new weapons and techniques for Special Operations personnel under his control as was the late Captain John Beauchamp of the Lincoln County Sheriff's Department. Judge Shawn McCarver's life experiences have taken him away from Special Operations, but his many insights into firearms and tactics are always appreciated and helpful and the Bench's gain has been the Special Operations world's loss.

While others have helped me in preparing this work, naturally only I can take the blame for any shortcomings. My usual test for a book I write is whether or not it would be a work that I would like to read – if so, then I think the work is useful. I would like to read this book and hopefully you will also.

What is a Special Operator? Chapter 1

Obviously, Special Operations are conducted by Special Operators. The question thus becomes who is a Special Operator? What are the characteristics of such a person? How and why is he different from the standard military man or police officer? I spoke with my friend Leroy Thompson, who is one of the world's leading authorities in this area, and his opinion was that if you asked 50 knowledgeable people about the subject, you would likely get 50 different answers. Perhaps, but this, of course, does not solve my problem of properly defining the term so we do not get lost or side-tracked as we proceed on our course of inquiry pertaining to weapons' tactics and training of the Special Operator.

I come to this field as an ex-infantry officer who was a "straight leg" (non-airborne qualified) man. I was not a Special Forces Operative. Later as a federal law enforcement agent, I ran a police department of over 40 men who conducted 24-hours-a-day 7-days-a-week work, and, while I created and trained a specialist response unit to conduct raids resulting in arrests and hostage rescue, for the most part the work was of the standard dull routine patrol/watchman type activity. Mundane, true, but critically important to the vast majority of people in the serviced community.

I note this to make it clear that I have no special axe to grind in this subject area, preferring no one group over another. As an ex-straight leg infantryman, I suppose I would say that Special Operators do things that standard troops do not do. Not that they could not do them (for a true US infantryman can do anything if given the training, equipment, and leadership), but the Special Operator comes to the task with the training and equipment already in hand to perform the task and does not need to be brought up to speed.

Hence, for example, a combat patrol forward of your position, performed by a rifle company, would not be a Special Operation in my judgment, for it is a task any rifleman can be expected to perform, albeit potentially very dangerous. While a long-range, behind-the-lines-extended-duration-patrol seeking intelligence about the enemy, hoping to avoid any enemy activity, calls for better or at least different skills and equipment, and it may in fact be much safer to perform than a standard combat patrol a mile or so in front of your position.

Similarly battle in built-up areas can be conducted by standard infantry troops. These battles can be very dangerous and require a lot of skill in managing small units and coordinating actions. No one familiar with the urban battlefields of Hue, Vietnam, in 1968 can doubt the danger involved. But the skills necessary to deploy into an urban area and snatch an intended target from among friends, such as the Delta Team attempted in Somalia a few years back, call for greater training and different as well as better equipment. Both are equally dangerous actions. In fact, in this type of action as well as others, the standard infantryman in a "straight" leg unit is likely much more at risk than the Special Operator. I have always maintained that a person is safest with the most highly trained, elite unit assigned to what are perceived to be high-risk, critical assignments. They tend to have better equipment, better plans, better-trained soldiers, and are not confronted with the daily meat-grinder deadness found in standard units. Nor are such units the frequent targets of constantly pounding artillery, the true killer on the battlefield at any time period.

So it is also with police work. The highly trained and equipped SWAT (Special Weapons & Tactics) team member in all honesty is much less at risk than the rural sheriff's deputy answering the domestic relations call at the remote mobile home location at 9:00 pm on a Saturday night. The SWAT team member is trained and equipped to conduct missions that the standard deputy could possibly learn to handle but comes to the task pre-trained and equipped. It is not the willingness to accept danger that makes the SWAT officer a Special Operator: it is the specialized equipment and training.

Glamour must thus not be considered when discussing the Special Operator. Nor should the idea that, somehow, their men are braver than their colleagues. Nor that they face a greater risk in their actions. None of these is true. What is true is that the Special Operator will need special skills and equipment to perform unusual or one-time tasks and that the Special Operator will come to this task already trained and equipped to perform it. He will not need to learn the skills on the job or make do with equipment that may be less suitable to the task than can be obtained.

It is this equipment and training that we will study hereafter, not the individuals who utilize it.

Chapter 2

A short history of Special Operations

While it could be said that Special Operations and those who conduct them have been with us as long as military deployments (and later policing) existed, perhaps only in the last 175 years or so have the Special Operators been distinguished by their choice of weapons, frequently using cutting-edge technological weapons, which is one of their defining characteristics.

When Captain Jack Hays led his band of 15 Texas Rangers against some 80 or more Comanche Indians in the late 1830s, he was acting as a Special Operator. He went well beyond the limits of a standard infantryman or dragoon of the period and his special skill in handling the newly developed revolver from atop his "hay burner" allowed him and his associates to rout the Indians and forever changed plains warfare. Whereas previously the horse-mounted Comanche almost always overcame their infantry opponents and normally would defeat an equal number of dragoons armed with single-shot rifles and handguns, here Captain Hays and his men successfully overcame a force almost six times their size. Specialized training and special equipment made the day for them.

During the US Civil War, simply armed cavalry units on both sides often

Members of the Boer Commandos pose in the field.

Special Operations: weapons & tactics

The author with M191B Bergman SMG equipped with a Luger snail drum. This was the choice of World War I German Storm Troopers – early day special operators.

penetrated deep behind enemy lines and, carrying upwards of six revolvers, did battle with many times their number of standard infantry troops, defeating them readily. These deep-penetrating Cavalry men armed with the most modern of weapons were every bit as much a Special Operator as today's Delta Team member who lands behind enemy lines to seize prisoners, destroy vital links in enemy communications, or conduct other operations.

During the Boer War at the turn of the 20th century, horse-mounted Boer Commando Units penetrated deeply into British-held territory and destroyed vital communications and supply depots as well as keeping enough pressure on the British to force them to deploy many troops to catch them which could have otherwise been used at the more traditional front-line operations. These Commandos, like the men who were to take their name in World War II, were fine marksmen, better trained than the normal soldier of the period, and capable of traveling long distances rapidly thanks to their selection of horseflesh and riding skills. The Boer Commando member riding behind enemy lines (whether 15 years old or 70 or anywhere in between) was every bit as much a Special Operator as any man from the Special Air Service today.

World War I (1914–18) is frequently thought about in terms of static trench warfare with the infantry huddled down in open trenches, sustaining artillery barrage after artillery barrage broken only from time to time with a mad, massive charge over the top, only to be mowed down by the enemy's machine gun. Unfortunately it was that way for many, but even in the trenches of World War I there were Special Operators. Those individuals who stripped off their helmets, gas masks, and heavy clothes and who, armed with bayonet, club, grenade and handgun, went over the top conducting trench raids to gather intelligence, capture prisoners, or perhaps on occasion merely to keep up their offensive spirit were every bit as much a Special Operator as a Soviet Spetnaz trooper. They developed special skills and used special equipment to accomplish tasks that could not be performed by a line infantryman.

Trench raiders existed on both sides of the line, of course, although most of us are more familiar with British, Canadian, US and other English-speakers' (and writers') actions but the other combatants all used the same skills and equipment to accomplish the same thing.

The Germans, however, brought to the war in the last several months what clearly has to be considered a Special Operator, the Storm Trooper. These soldiers were traditional infantrymen trained to a somewhat higher standard, possibly equipped with the newly developed Bergman M1918 SMG (although there is some debate on this point) as well as the Maxim 08/15 LMG, to give them greater short-range fire power and an ability to carry aggressive attacks to the allies. While they did not conduct intelligence-gathering operations by virtue of their specialized training, skills and weapons, they almost turned the tide of the war in fact. I suppose all of us who read these words can be happy that they did not arrive in 1917 before the massive infusion of fresh US troops rendered their attacks ineffective.

The author firing a MG08115 LMG.

Members of the Shanghai International Settlement Riot Squad run for their waiting vehicles in this photograph dating to the 1920s.

With the war over in 1918 the military went back into a period of decay. Special Operators are rarely if ever "the fair-haired lads" of any army, and those who gravitate to such units typically find themselves left behind in promotions if not actually out on the street when the hostilities cease. Interestingly enough during this interwar period, the main field of development in Special Operations techniques took place far from the center of military might and in a very unexpected place, namely the Police Force of the Shanghai International Settlement. The Shanghai International Settlement Police consisted at the time of some 9,000 officers, mainly Chinese but with some Indian and European officers also. Shanghai, in the International Settlement, was a densely packed urban area with a teeming population and a serious criminal element in the Green Gang, who smuggled drugs and conducted kidnapping for ransom as common business propositions. The criminal class was often well armed with serious military-style weapons and, due to the potential for a successful flight to an adjoining jurisdiction, thereby depriving the International Settlement Police of jurisdiction, was often quite willing and capable of seriously resisting arrest.

Confronted with such groups, the firearms and tactics section found that the traditional methods employed in the pre-1911 years, when China was stable to a great degree, patterned to a large extent on British policing methods, were no longer were successful. Far too many armed encounters ended with a dead or injured constable and a criminal who successfully fled the scene. It was into this void that William Fairbairn, who was at the time a musketry instructor, stepped. He developed a new training scheme based on the reality of the

Chapter 2: A short history of Special Operations

William Fairbairn of the Shanghai Municipal Police and SOE showing him as an instructor firing with the M1 Thompson 45 ACP SMG.

streets of Shanghai and taught the officers how to successfully engage in the street battles they encountered. No armchair tactician, Fairbairn is reported to have responded personally to over 200 armed incidents. Naturally, this does not mean he engaged in 200 gunfights, merely responded in one way or another to over 200 incidents. It is known, however, that Fairbairn did engage in a few gun battles during raids he personally conducted.

While training individual officers and raiding teams was important, Fairbairn also created the first SWAT-type team in existence. While perhaps a simplification to say it, Shanghai was a hotbed of Communist and Union organizing in the years prior to 1937 as well as having a serious criminal underworld which had more or less political connections with the Chinese Nationalist government after 1927. When such entities resisted the efforts of the International Settlement Police, something better was called for than a few stick- and handgun-armed constables. Fairbairn's answer was to develop the

Special Operations: weapons & tactics

BA British commando in training early in World War II.

Riot Squad. It was perhaps there that Fairbairn first encountered Eric Anthony Sykes whom he partnered in developing the famous fighting knife that bears both their names. Both gentlemen returned to England in 1940 and immediately joined the training division of the British military giving the commando and later both the British Special Operation Executive (SOE) and US Office of Strategic Services (OSS) the benefits of their years of experience in the streets of Shanghai. Those hard-won lessons in Shanghai street battles where, apparently, occasional house-to-house fighting with hand-held automatic weapons, sniping rifles and even Mills Bombs (grenades) took place, were re-taught at such places as London's Street Fighting School in the 1940s to the benefit of allied soldiers.

During World War II, a large number of organizations on the allied side developed what must be acknowledged to be Special Operations methods. Whether the British Army Commandos, who were charged with raids to help maintain the aggressive spirit in a time of general defeat and to gain intelligence as well as tie down large numbers of German soldiers, or units like

Greek guerrillas photographed on Crete participating in the kidnapping of a German general, led by SOE officers: a very fine Special Operation.

A French 'commando' in training with a Fairbairn Sykes knife in World War II.

Realistic training is always an important objective: these US Army Rangers are training during World War II.

the Long Range Desert Reconnaissance Group, these men all clearly met our definition of a Special Operator. During the Desert Campaign, the archetypal Special Operator developed when David Stirling managed to convince the British military to permit him to develop the Special Air Service. At the time, of course, no one knew exactly what this was to be or do but Stirling and the other founders soon created a lot of opportunities for their lethal talents.

Naturally other allied forces were not to be left out and almost all the Western Allied countries developed their own Commando or SAS-style units. The French in particular were particularly keen on the issue and well-equipped to perform the functions of deep-penetration intelligence gathering and destruction as well as assisting indigenous peoples resist invaders. The US of course developed their Ranger program modeled on the Commando pattern and, to this day, the US Army Rangers represent some of the finest Special Operators around, being generally the starting point for even more exotic Special Operations groups like the Special Forces and Delta.

The Germans developed Special Operators later, possibly because their early successes in the field made many traditional German military men shun such unusual units. Of course, no doubt the German army was like every other traditional military organization, where conventional military leaders frequently dislike Special Operations Units as they feel with some justification that they tend to attract the best soldiers away, utilize a disproportionate share of the scarcest resources and rarely are equipped heavily enough to really maintain the ground they seize initially.

The early use of parachute-delivered German infantrymen was an

Trainers at OSS Camp in World War II. On the top row, fourth from the left, is Rex Applegate, and on the front row, second from the the right in a dark uniform, is William Fairbairn.

exception to the traditional German military position, and the losses sustained on Crete confirmed the opinions of many in the High Command that they were not effective. This inability to hold the ground initially seized in the face of a determined traditional infantry counterattack is, unfortunately, a problem and thus airborne units can only be justified by the ability of such units to perform tasks immediately that would take normal units quite a bit of time to get trained for, assuming that they could accomplish that level of training. It is only fair to recognize that while most units (and individuals) could be brought up to a higher standard with greater time and training, it is nevertheless true that some people are better in certain areas by reason of reflexes and interest level; so that a unit composed of such individuals will always be better than one composed of a more heterogeneous grouping of soldiers. This is no doubt especially true in a war-time, mainly draftee army.

The German Special Operator Skorzeny perhaps best represents the German Special Operator. He certainly was up to the skill and daring of any allied Special Operations man, and possibly faced greater obstacles among his supervisors than, at least, the British, who had Churchill always using such daring Special Operations much to the disgust frequently of conventional British military thinkers. Skorzeny's raid to rescue Mussolini from his Italian captors in a mountain top hotel is perhaps the finest example of a Special Operations action in his wartime record of daring deeds.

In Asia, Special Operations were also busy in such places as Burma, where deep-penetration raids by Wingate and Merrill took place and could, I believe, fairly be considered Special Operations. More typical might be the actions of

Marine raiders on Bougainville dug in on the beach. Note the Reising SMG carried by the man in the foreground.

the OSS with the Kacin guerilla groups in Burma. Then they acted as force multipliers and tied up a large body of Japanese troops. The island campaigns did not lead themselves to Special Operations very much, although occasionally they did, and episodes such as in the Philippines, where US troops dropped into Japanese-held territory to rescue prisoners before they could be executed or removed by the Japanese, might qualify for the term. Similarly the beach reconnaissance conducted by UDT (Underwater Demolition Team) teams might fairly be thought of as Special Operations. China, which would have seemed an ideal area for Special Operations on the OSS model in Burma, effectively was a non-starter during the war due to the unwillingness of the Nationalist Chinese government to permit US military operations of that type to be seriously conducted.

When World War II ended, many of the Special Operations groups were quickly disbanded, deemed unnecessary in the post-atomic era and, as noted earlier, considered too expensive in terms of draining off the best manpower and using too many resources for what they accomplished in reality compared with what they *proposed* to accomplish. In the US, Ranger units were disbanded, and in the British service, the Commandos were similarly broken up as Army special units with the Marines being tasked with the same

duties. Of course, the OSS units were also dissolved as was the SAS in the English military.

Events have a way of occurring that people are unable to anticipate at times, however, and the Chinese Communists, who had so successfully fought the Japanese in Malaya during the war, were not willing to go back to being rural workers and allowing the British to retain their colony once the Japanese were gone. Soon the British found that their soldiers were no better at fighting the Chinese guerillas in Malaya than the Japanese had been, at least until hard-won lessons were appreciated and implemented at a general level. The SAS was reborn in Malaya and proved itself to be a remarkable military formation there and in other actions around the world in the next half century.

In the US, the confrontation with the Soviet Union and later Communist China led first to the development of heavy mechanical conventional military formations ready to fight in the plains of central Europe or on the Chinese mainland. But it soon became obvious to many that a behind-the-lines guerilla unit of people who were opposed to the Communist could be very valuable. Based on the success of such training teams during World War II, the US Army Special Forces was reborn. Soon the real risk was Communist insurgence in poor countries where the military was weak and unable to cope with such unconventional warfare activities. The US Special Forces Units could deploy to those areas and on one hand teach these government's conventional military units how to successfully fight Communist guerilla groups and also

French Foreign legionnaires such as these in Vietnam handled many Special Operations in the period up to 1954.

Special Operations: weapons & tactics

Troopers of the US Special Forces practice their field survival skills in this photograph of the 1950s.

help arm and train local groups who wanted to oppose such Communist guerilla groups who brought terror to the countryside. Thus from being guerilla trainers, the Special Forces transformed themselves into guerilla fighters over a period of time. While it was originally seen as a key goal to train local people how to use these methods to oppose the Communist guerillas, unfortunately, apart from in Southeast Asia where the Special Forces had a pretty free hand for a long period, most of their time was spent training conventional military units of governments, sadly all too often despotic, how to oppose guerilla fighters who were sometimes fronts for Communist groups and sometimes not.

During the Vietnam War, the US Army Special Forces trained many villagers, ran a successful mercenary army in both Laos and Vietnam and also conducted deep raids into the entire area. It is, I believe, fair to say that their work at all levels, including the SOG (Study & Observation Group) teams, can legitimately claim to be Special Operations.

While the US was busy in Vietnam and elsewhere in the world confronting Communist-sponsored guerilla groups in the period 1954 to 1975, as the Vietnam War played out, and African Wars of Liberation ground down to what can be viewed as conventional civil wars between dissimilar groups thrust together by Europeans in the 19th century, another threat arose on the world stage that was also to be used by a response by the Special Operator, namely terrorist actions.

Israeli commandos place a demo charge in this pre-1967 photograph.

Of course, terrorists have always been with us and certainly the period of 1880 to 1914 was notable for the number of terrorist incidents which occurred in Europe sponsored by Socialists, Communists and anarchist groups. Such actions seem to die out with the beginning of World War I in 1914 for a variety of reasons. Of course, there were occasionally some terrorist acts in Western Europe, generally off-shoots of Balkan activities, and Ireland remained an area of major concern for England during the period.

In the late 1960s, terrorism again became a popular technique for otherwise weak groups to get attention for their causes and to inflict damages and costs on their opponents far in excess of the costs to themselves. There were many reasons for this, including: the rise of anti-US sentiment in Europe due to the Vietnam War, anti-establishment sentiment in France due to their education system which led to the 1968 student revolts, the 1967 Arab-Israeli War when the Israelis launched a war against the Arabs seizing much territory, the existence of safe havens in Eastern Europe where the Soviet Union held sway and determined that chaos in the West was a benefit to their aim of achieving worldwide domination and the realization of Arab and other oil producing states that they were wealthy and could impact the West by using the tools of world terrorism.

Initially attempts to meet this latest wave of European terrorism were disappointing. Much as Fairbairn found out in the 1920s in Shanghai, conventional watchman-style police agencies were not capable of dealing with this threat and the military of the countries was not capable of performing a policing role either. When the police efforts proved too feeble and the military efforts too ineffective, it became time to develop the Special Counterterrorist operator. In Europe this took on the approach of training the police up to the tasks presented or establishing a special military unit to perform the function. Of course, the issue often resulted in a blended approach as obviously political considerations were paramount and many political battles were fought in "turf wars."

The key to counterterrorist operations seems to be to rapidly bring the ability to inflict great violence very selectively on small targets who are frequently surrounded by total innocents. This becomes critical because many of these incidents are played out on the front pages of newspapers or on TV. Additionally, thankfully, these incidents are quite rare, so on-the-job-training that might be available (albeit at some considerable human cost and risk) cannot be relied upon to either bring the men involved up to the requisite skill or maintain it. Training becomes critical. Additionally, certain specialized equipment is clearly useful to performing the unique tasks presented. This equipment is often very expensive both in terms of acquisition as well as skill maintenance costs and since it is needed so infrequently, it is not justifiable to train all men involved with general policing roles in its use or maintenance, nor, of course, could all of them learn or necessarily have the proper inclination to use it. Additionally, it must be acknowledged, especially at the sharpest end, these duties are those best conducted by a seasoned, mature but not old man as physical conditioning can become a major issue in some operations.

Today, almost every country of the world has specialized units tasked with counterterrorist activities. Often a large number of organizations exist with overlapping powers and abilities but all are fairly called Special Operations for under our definition they are trained to a higher level of skill and tasked with performing a type of duty immediately that would require additional training for the standard police officer or soldier and could under certain circumstances be beyond their skills.

Marksmanship/tactical training techniques

Chapter 3

I believe we can take it as a given that any person who is likely to be involved with a Special Operations team will have elementary marksmanship skills and safety issues before they show up. Whether learned at training academies, or, preferably, in the field by virtue of pre-service interest in shooting, the Special Operator should not need to be taught simple marksmanship. Instead the issues with such programs geared to Special Operations units, whether military or civilian, should be concerned with skill refinement (the ability to shoot smaller groups), increasing the shooter's speed in shooting (smaller groups are good but faster is always better as long as the target is critically struck), and, perhaps most importantly, judgment. A shot that goes wrong can have lasting effects both to the organization generally, the individual member (whether civil/criminal or psychological) and the mission itself at times. All proper programs should encourage proper judgment being exercised before making the shot.

It is also important to introduce stress into any problem so the members can calculate how they will act when confronted with the real thing. While it is obviously impossible to totally include the proper stress level to duplicate actual combat, a proper training program can come very close, and even surpass, certain aspects of real combat. For instance, it has been said often that training at the US Ranger course is often more difficult than participating in actual combat from a physical standpoint. Especially in military teams, a willingness to accept certain injuries in training to help minimize injuries in combat can be clearly accepted. It is unfortunately more difficult to justify these things in police-type training but the trainer should strive to get it to the proper level without exposing the participants to useless hazards as opposed to useful hazards. To use an example of what I mean, Col. Rex Applegate once told me of the training conducted at the Commando School in Scotland during World War II. It, of course, was important to train people to stay down lest they get shot. The training cadre would, when they spotted a commando trainee exposing himself, fire a .303 Enfield at them aiming about three feet high. The crack of the passing bullet was to remind them to get down. They then would rapidly reload and fire the next round where the person had been standing. If down, no harm was done. If not, they would get killed or injured. A tough way to remind everyone to stay down but no doubt the training saved more lives than it took, which the Colonel said was 16. It may have been more, or perhaps less, as Colonal Applegate's memory may have been faulty, and there is really no way to know for certain today as I assume reports in the 1940s involving training fatalities as were as often "doctored" as they are today. But it was a good number and no incredible rarity. It's fairly easy to justify such training with a military Special Operations unit. A lot of what they do will be at the edge of the envelope anyway but it is the best way to learn. Many times proper training may be more dangerous than the actual event. Flying at night, low, with starlight goggles on, is dangerous. But if you want to be able to use the tactics, you must practice it. So it is with firearms

27

Using the MP5: the author demonstrates the use of a sling. Once the SMG is emptied, it is quicker to drop it rather than waste time reloading. The sling allows the weapon to hang from the chest, so it does not get lost, and enables the shooter to engage the target with a Beretta DAO pistol. This technique is faster than reloading the SMG but requires practice if it is to be mastered.

training. If you want guys to be able to move forward while people provide covering fire, they must practice it. Similarly with entering a building where the enemy awaits: in the real world, men will be in front of and behind you with loaded weapons poised to shoot. So it must be training. In the real world, you will wear all of your field gear and carry spare ammo. So you must in training. In the real world, you will deploy in hot weather and cold, rain and snow. So you must conduct your training. Better to learn that your gloves will get behind the trigger of your weapon tying it up on a training session than on the street.

Training injuries are typically much harder to justify in the police Special Operations field. There you are faced with civil liability concerns and adverse publicity if someone gets hurt. Not that such matters do not raise their heads in military Special Operations groups, but somehow it seems more reasonable

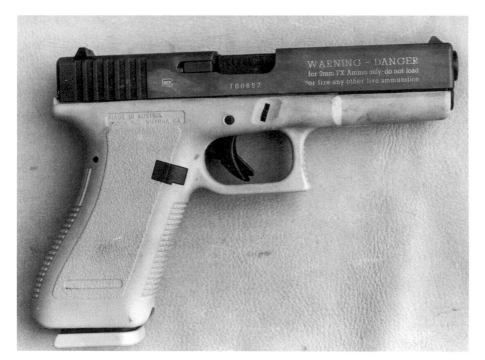

Right-side view of the Glock 17T. Note the warnings on the slide and the receiver, which is blue in colour.

Left-side view of the Glock 17T. Note the special chambering for the 9mm FX cartridge.

9 mm Simunition rounds used in the Glock 17T. Red and blue paint rounds are available. (Not to scale.)

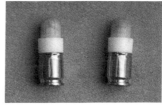

if a person gets hurt who is a soldier in training than if he is a policeman.

The key element here is the recognition that to be really realistic in training we must accept a degree of injury potential. You cannot train someone to be a jet-fighter pilot using simulators or flying trainers alone. Ultimately they must fly state-of-the-art fighters at the edge of the envelope. When you do that, some people will crash and burn. You hope that the number is minimal and

Special Operations: weapons & tactics

The military sniper shown here in training has different goals and tactics from his civilian counterpart.

you take solace from the fact that the benefits at the training stage are such that in actual combat the lives saved by the training outweigh the lives lost in training; yet it is still hard on the spouses and orphans of the pilot who died in training. Safety in training is good but it is not an end all by any means.

The ability to refine marksmanship skill typically comes from repeating the actions under the direction of someone who already knows how to get the maximum benefit from certain methods. For instance, practice in squeezing the trigger, focusing on the sights, and similar tasks will improve the shooter's skill by familiarity. Certain types of positions are known to produce better results. A proper use of the sitting position for instance will yield better results than a poor sitting position. Proper training and practice will improve the shooter's ability to load and operate his weapon. All of these tasks will improve or refine the Special Operator's ability to place bullets into small groups. When you consider that, at least in my experience, you can plan on shooting about twice as well on the range as you do in real life, this type of refinement is important. Instead of a four-inch group at, say, 200 yards you refine your technique to get two inches. Then in a real-life encounter, you will be able to hit the four-inch target at 200 yards rather than miss it, since your group is now eight inches in reality. Of course, the goal is to be able to shoot the weapon from all positions to the limit of the weapon and ammunition. Occasionally this may occur but take it from me, it will not be too frequently.

With this refinement matter discussed, let me make it clear that a Special Operation group is not a match shooting team. We want them to be able to shoot their weapons accurately and at a distance. The latter will make it safe for them, especially in police work where their opponents typically but not always have marginal skills which can be limited by distance between the offender and the officer. The former of course is an obvious benefit clearly understood. But we also want the Special Operator to be fast: fast both in presenting his weapon (whether holstered or shouldered), firing his first and subsequent shots *and* shooting at all targets presented, since multiple targets can be expected to be the norm in many situations.

The Special Operator gets the ability to shoot fast by repetition of the actual shooting and by using the methods determined to increase the speed in presentation by removing all those acts which take time and do nothing to improve the presentation. Practice in firing multiple shots will train the Special Operator to rapidly recover from recoil and to take the steps necessary to get proper weapon alignment and trigger usage. We obviously do not want the operator to go so fast that he misses but we do want them to fire as fast as possible, consistent with the accuracy needed in a particular situation. At three yards, for instance, two shots in four inches may be quite acceptable in one-quarter second; that same ratio at 200 yards is about 23 feet, hardly sufficient but two shots in three seconds into four inches at 200 yards is quite good but way too slow at three yards. We must know the possibles to determine whether the operator is getting to the limits of nature We all know Ed McGivern could shoot five clay birds in the air at once with a .38 S&W four-inch M&P-style revolver. That's excellent work! Hitting one is not incredibly difficult with a degree of practice. Hitting two takes a lot more effort, but has hardly gotten into the envelope, obviously. I do not expect anyone to shoot an off-hand group of five shots at 200 yards with a handgun that goes into six inches but hitting a man target each time for five shots at 200 yards with a handgun is not expecting too much nor is expecting it to be done in 10 seconds. It all depends on the situation.

Whatever the situation and weapon type, it is critical that the tasks presented to the Special Operator be done at the fastest rate possible. Things happen fast in the real world so the faster the operator can shoot accurately at his target the better as it exposes him to less reaction time by his opponent and most critically gives him more time to make judgments about shooting itself.

For it is this last point that is the most critical element of training for the Special Operator – whether civilian or military – *learning when to shoot and when not to shoot*. No bullet can be called back once fired. Every time you fire your weapon you must be prepared emotionally, economically, legally and tactically for the consequences of your shot. This calls for training in judgment-making as otherwise you will freeze and be unable to function or make a proper decision.

Judgment-making is a skill that can be developed by exposing the operator to certain factual situations that are commonly encountered in the field, then allowing him to rapidly evaluate the stimuli to come to a decision. He must be taught to rapidly pick out critical factors that assist in making determinations and then learn to rapidly act upon the conclusions reached. Naturally some people will be better at doing this than others, and some people are capable of decision-making faster than others also. Even if some people are faster and some slower, everyone tends to get better with practice. If they get worse as they discover they are so overloaded with stimuli that they are unable to make a quick decision, then they have no business on your team and must go elsewhere. Naturally the more rapid the analysis and decision-making the greater the likelihood that wrong decisions will be made, but you must recognize that making no decision is also a decision and very frequently that clearly will be the wrong decision.

This area of decision-making training when linked with firearms training is an area where certain training tools come in very handy. For instance, laser-sighted units installed in weapons that actuate spots on the target or person to simulate a hit (MILES (Multiple Integrated Laser Engagement System) units in the military) are quite handy. This will help tell whether a trainee fired his weapon and hit the target. Similarly in police and close-quarter battle drills, simulations which project a paint-filled capsule from standard duty-type weapons modified slightly to fire the cartridge are excellent training tools. They inflict a certain pain penalty and clearly mark the opponent with strikes. The drawback is that 25 yards seems to be about the maximum range they can be effectively used for military purposes and in some civilian Special Operations purposes this is too short a distance. The MILES units do not suffer this range limitation but do require a special unit to be utilized, are more expensive to purchase, and do not provide any pain penalty. In past days, other types of simulations have been used from BB-guns to wax bullets such as were used in Dr Devilliers's cartridges at the mid-to-end of the 19th century. Of course, with any such simulated loads, you must train with them in the proper mind-set otherwise you get situations where people will attack as they are willing to accept a paint capsule to the chest and its attendant pain to achieve their goal when they never would accept a 9 mm to the chest. Blank cartridges are also sometimes used in mock fighting but really bring little realism to the task.

Using your standard weapon and ammo is always the best but, of course, it is difficult to avoid sterile training sessions. One way to accomplish this is to use a cinema range. At these ranges, a film scenario is exhibited on the screen which then has to be shot by the person using a real weapon with real ammo hopefully (although both laser guns and plastic ammunition used in real weapons are also sometimes used) These ranges are excellent training tools, combining all the three elements we want to develop. The key is to have a large number of scenario variations, so the trainee does not memorize the proper responses, and to make the filmed scenarios realistic. Ideally, for police agencies, they should be filmed in the local area using up-to-date cars, dress for the actors and street scenes. Occasionally you see movies that are now quite vintage and I believe the trainee may very well be spending a lot of time viewing the vintage film as vintage film rather than as an actual real-life event. The training is thus degraded. Military units can also use such filmed scenarios, but it is a bit more difficult to get proper films as much military-style operations may take place at night and at greater distances than is common in police operations. Still, with some effort, some really excellent training films can be prepared. Recently, objects that will fire back at the engaged shooter on the video range have been developed which will encourage the shooter to take proper cover. Without such things, it's critical that the trainer see to it that the trainee adopt proper cover and concealment techniques when training on the video range lest this important element be lost.

Among the aspects of weapons training for Special Operations personnel, whether military or civil, any proper training program should include foreign (or non-issued at least) weapons. This is, of course, easier with military units who are likely to encounter certain standard weapons in the hands of the opponents than the wide variety of weapons found in civil situation. If the Special Operators are expected to operate worldwide, then the net must be cast wide but it is still not likely to be as wide as that necessary for civil Special Operators.

This training should include both familiarization for safety purposes as well as training in shooting of the weapons. This is a tall order: a US Special Operator in the military should be able to operate, fire and maintain all Soviet-patterned standard weapons in use since 1941 *and* be familiar to the same level with US/Allied patterns in use over the same period of time. Civilian teams need to be similarly familiar, if only at the safety level rather than firing or maintenance (although that would be useful also and help to keep up interest), so that if they encounter a weapon at a scene, they will not pick it up and accidentally shoot themselves. Don't laugh – it has happened and was once so common with officers encountering MAC-10 open-bolt SMG in Miami that a ballistic bag to place them in to make them safe to handle, since they were incapable of unloading them safely, was developed by Richard Davis of Second Chance Safety Vest fame. Not only are such classes quite useful in the event the operator encounters odd weapons, whether they become stranded and need to use them for actual fighting purposes or merely to render them safe to handle (as souvenirs or evidence) but also they are interesting to most people who are attracted to Special Operation groups and gives them a feeling that they are special. This is always a useful thing as it keeps morale up which will help get such people through the hard times which are sure to come in any Special Operations group.

Throughout all of the training it is essential that the training must be relatively interesting and, I believe, fun. People will not spend time doing things that are not fun. If it is fun, they will look forward to the training and do well at it. If they view it as a drudgery, they will attempt to avoid it, do as little as possible, and have a poor attitude towards the entire situation. When I was in the Army originally, I looked forward to going shooting, for I came to the Army as someone who was very interested in shooting and weapons. To my shock, I soon found out that no one in the Army liked to go shooting and I soon found out why – it was not fun! Now it does not have to be easy to be fun, in fact the more difficult something is to accomplish the more fun it is in retrospect. Nor does the weather have to be nice to make a fun day. What it needs to be is fun. You can make training fun if the instructors teach with skill and politeness. It will be fun if the trainee is treated with respect and if they realize they are learning something of value. Think back to classes you have taken at intervals. Some were fun; some were not. A Special Operations trainer must make certain his training is fun. When I first started running firearms training programs in the Army, I soon learned how to tell if the classes were done properly: if the students wanted to stay and talk after the class was over. If not, they were eager to leave. Naturally you always will have someone who will "sour grapes" anything (I once had someone file a union grievance against me as my M16 class kept them four minutes over shift change) but this is generally a good rule. A Special Operations trainer for an agency should remember people pay their own money and spend their own free time to go take classes with Col. Cooper at Gunsite and Clint Smith at Thunder Ranch, just to name two schools, popular in the US as well as worldwide. Your classes should be as good, interesting and fun and if so, your students will learn what you have to teach them rapidly and completely.

Military v. police Special Operations   Chapter 4

Military and Police Special Operations Teams and activities vary considerably. One could almost go so far as to say there are frequently more dissimilarities than the contrary. This is an interesting issue, for too many people (even those serving on teams) confuse the two and believe they are the same or nearly so. This is a mistake unless you live in that part of the world where the government is run by a military dictatorship willing to impose its martial authority on all the inhabitants of the country. I do not live in such a place, do not want to live in such a place, and have no intention of living in such a place. I would imagine most readers would feel the same.

Possibly the most important points separating the two involve the legal basis for their operating and the restrictions this imposes on them. Men assigned to Special Operations groups must understand these legal under-pinnings and guide their actions accordingly. Failure to do so will place them in serious legal jeopardy, if not at that particular moment then later when a new group of political leaders comes to power. And a new group will always come to power to review and criticize the actions you undertook under their predecessors in office, unless you are already dead. Thus if you act outside your limits, you should anticipate problems down the road, criminal, civil, or administrative, while if you act within the legal limits of your power, you will have minimal concerns later.

Military teams are limited by the International Law of War and all that it entails. This means that no Special Operations group may conduct operations that run foul of the law of war any more than any standard military unit can. If you are assigned to, or you are a voluntary member of, such a military Special Operations unit, you must refuse to engage in any operation that would expose you to liability. If you are involved in such unlawful operations, urge a change in policy or quit. We all know following orders is not a legitimate excuse.

What are some typical actions that are prohibited by the Law of War?

1 Using weapons or ammunition designed to cause unnecessary suffering. This is a difficult issue at times and many people tend to laugh at it, saying if you can drop napalm on a subject, why not use hollow-point expanding ammunition. The argument is interesting but does not settle the issue. Typically this issue comes up regarding expanding ammunition and its use in a military environment. Merely having a hole in the top of the bullet jacket is not enough as some hollow points, such as Federal Match/Military Match in the US Service, have a hole in the top of the bullet jacket due to the way the bullet is constructed but it is not designed to expand and thus is not a prohibited cartridge. Other loads such as buckshot are not designed to expand and may be similarly used but some rounds are meant to expand and they are prohibited.

2 Actions may not be taken that will inflict unnecessary civilian suffering. If there is a way to minimize civilian casualties and still accomplish a legitimate military objective, you must follow it. This frequently comes up with the taking of civilian hostages or bombing villages suspected of

Special Operations: weapons & tactics

The author firing a suppressed Ingram M-10 in 1979: an excellent 'low-profile' weapon for special operations teams in urban areas.

harboring enemy soldiers when it is not known for certain where they are. Both are prohibited.

3 It is unlawful to poison water and food supplies. This is often done in guerilla campaigns to limit the guerillas' access to food by killing them with poison or making them decline to use available stocks.

4 It is improper to torture individuals for information. This was a commonly ignored prohibition in Vietnam. Typically, US officers would allow their Vietnamese counterparts to torture captured subjects. While a concern to get information is understandable, it is simply unacceptable and illegal. Whether standard "grunt" or "Special Operator" such actions are illegal and justify long periods in prison.

5 Actions that are disproportionate to ends sought are also illegal. Blowing

A rare photograph of a British sniper in Northern Ireland, armed with a L42A1. This photograph was taken in 1972 at the height of 'The Troubles' in the New Lodge area of Belfast. Note the 'Scout Regiment' telescope still in use after 70 years!

up an entire block of an enemy town to get one enemy soldier is disproportionate and hence illegal.

There is a wide variety of other acts that likewise fall afoul of the International Law of War. Anyone who serves in a military unit of any sophistication should have had a class on the law of war long before they became a member of the Special Operations team. The applicability of the law does not change merely because you wear a special hat or call yourself a special name. Whether German infantrymen or SS man, British Tommy or SAS, US grunt (standard infantryman) or Delta Team operative, the International Law of War must guide your actions. You get no more leeway merely because of your special position and, in fact, it might be fair to say you should be held to a higher standard, because you are probably a more carefully trained and mature soldier, expected to understand the law and being experienced in military matters to a higher degree than a junior military man.

Civilian Special Operations team act under even greater restraints than military teams. In most countries of the world, the Special Operators in a civilian context certainly have no more authority than any police officer and in most situations, police officers have no greater power than any other citizen. Of course, they may have different weapons and be given authority to conduct operations in a somewhat more aggressive nature but their ultimate authority is no greater. Depending on the law in the country where they are operating, they may be authorized to undertake certain actions that may be prohibited to a military Special Operator or use weapons and ammunition more effective then that permitted in the military.

A good example of this is the fact that the civilian Special Operator may typically use expanding ammunition designed to maximize stopping power by inflicting the maximum amount of injury on the target in the shortest period of time. The theory here, of course, is that the civilian Special Operator wants to stop the aggressive acts of his opponent as fast as possible to minimize the risk that such activities impose on the innocents in the community.

The civilian Special Operator can typically use deadly force only in certain, very limited situations. In the US, for instance, this is only when the lives of the operator or someone he is obligated to protect is placed in serious jeopardy of injury or death. In some countries, it is still permissible to use deadly force to effect the capture of an individual or prevent the individual's escape if a certain level of crime has been committed. That used to be the law in the US but not since the mid-1970s. The Special Operator can thus kill his opponent if that is the only way to stop the danger posed but is not authorized to do so merely because of the availability of the target, unlike his military counterpart.

The civilian Special Operator who exceeds his authority subjects himself to criminal as well as civil liability. This civil liability can be imposed on him personally not just on his employing agency. Similarly criminal sanctions may be imposed as a result of membership in the general group even if no personal action is undertaken by the operator himself. As this criminal and civil liability can follow many years after an event is over (and in the US can occur at different governmental levels – state and federal) any civilian Special Operator must be very careful not to overstep the mark. If directed by those in positions of authority to undertake actions that exceed those permitted (not just tactically unsound), the operator must decline to act. Just such a thing happened at a tactical deployment involving an alleged federal fugitive at Ruby Ridge in Idaho when supervisory FBI agents on the scene authorized deadly force in excess of what is permitted by law. Had the agents on the scene refused to act and walked off the assignment, not only would they have been spared much in the way of problems but also the agency itself would have been saved much dishonor. Rarely will any civilian Special Operator be criticized for using too little deadly force and you can be assured the opposite will not be the case.

The biggest risk that Special Operators have is police operators thinking they are military teams and military teams thinking they are exempt from the normal limitations placed on military units operating in the field. Neither is true. Civilian teams must take great care to always realize they operate with no more authority than the most humble of constables in their jurisdiction so far as legal authority is concerned and military teams must realize they are held to the same standard as any other military organization. Failure to keep these in mind will lead to unfortunate criminal and civil liability as well as tainting the Special Operations unit character and name of years to come both locally and otherwise. No mission, whether civil or military, is likely to be worth that cost.

Chapter 5

Analyzing your enemy

Tips to determine strengths and weaknesses

You often can tell much about your opponents by observing their weapons and the skills with which they handle them. Also, looking at how they are equipped may give you considerable insight into how proficient your enemies may be with their weapons.

I am writing this section in the aftermath of the airplane bombings of September 11, 2001, the US invasion of Afghanistan, operations in Yemen and on-going conflicts in Iraq. At first glance, there seems to be a large number of flinty-eyed guerilla warriors who are armed with AKM rifles and a plentiful supply of PK light machine guns and RPG-7 launchers who are brandishing them with great vigor. To anyone of my generation who had to plan on fighting the veteran warriors of North Vietnam's Army or the old line Viet Cong units, the prospect of another long-term guerilla campaign waged half a world away seems quite a task. One also remembers how support among the US civilian population seemed to disappear as the years went by and the thought obviously comes about how long the support will be there in the future for the current actions.

If you watch film clips closely, you will begin noticing things that you will also have observed, if thoughtful, from films of other troubled areas such as Yugoslavia or Africa. I hasten to point out that the observations that follow are not intended to denigrate any individuals' bravery or motivation. Many such people almost seem eager to die for their cause and this motivation may make them very dangerous foes but does nothing to make them more efficient warriors, technically speaking.

It is not at all uncommon to see in such areas the rear sight-leaf on the AKM rifle put in the 800-meter position. If you ask why, you will get the explanation that this makes the rifle more powerful and hence more deadly as, obviously, if the rifle will shoot further, it must be more powerful. Trajectory tables (and what they mean) seem not to be topic of large discussion in many areas. Obviously anyone who places his sights at 800 meters and then shoots at you when you are 300 meters or less away will shoot over you, even if he has a degree of skill, totally wasting his precious ammunition and not endangering you in the least. Naturally, not all of the warriors encountered are ignorant about ballistics, unfortunately, but quite a few who are will be encountered.

Another item rapidly picked up is the use of slings. The AKM rifle typically is equipped with a metal snap to slip on the front sling-mounting point and at the rear where the web sling is threaded through. Every photo I have seen lately shows them loosely flopping about. Obviously none of those "guerilla warriors" has ever gone on a night patrol that way. A trained person always tapes this sling down so it does not rattle, as he will other parts of the weapon which will rattle when moved. A rifle must pass the jump test if you are to take it to the field and not disclose your presence to your opponent. None in the photos I have seen is so fixed.

Another thing missing is pattern-painted finishes. In Vietnam, the distinctive 30-round magazine of the AK series in rifles frequently allowed US soldiers to spot the NVA/VC although he was otherwise not visible. Rifles like the AK (much less things like the M16A2) are quite distinctive in appearance and can be spotted by their regular appearance. As the Australians long ago showed with their factory-camouflaged, painted Owen SMG, a weapon to be used for fighting and not parade-ground work should be pattern-painted to break up the outline. I see no painted rifles/LMGs in the videos from overseas.

Other things amusingly missing are magazine pouches and web gear generally. These "guerilla warriors" who at least avail themselves of photo opportunities, carry no magazine pouches. A self-loading rifle (or actually any rifle) without spare ammunition immediately available is worthless after the initial load is fired. Whether in a chest-style pouch or a belt-mounted pouch, some spare ammunition must be carried if they are to prove to be an effective opponent.

If spare ammunition is carried, then look at the magazines themselves. Are the bottoms taped to avoid dropping a loaded one and the contents spilling out as the bottom sprays out? Do the magazines have a piece of cord (or better, a plastic magazine pull like Magpul) on it so it can be rapidly withdrawn from the pouch? If not, pulling them from the pouch is a time-consuming operation. If carried at all, are the magazines placed in the pouch ammunition down to protect the contents from the weather and make it faster to reload? If worn on a belt or at both sides, are the magazines placed so that the ammunition is placed in the correct position for faster loading into the weapon? Are the magazines numbered so the shooter can tell if one starts giving him problems so he can pitch it without confusion? Lastly, does the shooter carry some pouch to hold empty magazines in or will he drop them on the ground to be lost forever when he is done shooting them, with replacements soon to be found to be impossible to obtain?

In the same vein, do you see any cleaning equipment in evidence? While the AK/PK series of weapons will take a lot of abuse and keep firing, no weapon does its best dirty. A person who has the supplies necessary to maintain a weapon is likely to know more about weaponcraft than those who merely know how to make them go "bang."

If you see LMGs about, such as the PKM, see how they carry their spare ammunition. Is it on a belt slung around the neck, picking up all sorts of dirt and debris? If so, they should anticipate a lot of functioning problems. Most current LMGs have boxes to hold spare ammunition which can be mounted to the weapon to keep ammo and weapon together. People fail to use them at their own risk.

If you see handguns about, what types are they and how are they carried? If in flap-style holsters, you can figure they are likely only badges of office. If a person is seen to carry it in condition three (hammer down on an empty chamber) when it is a self-loader, you can be almost certain they are unfamiliar with handguns.

Are the people you observe young or old? Or perhaps middle-aged? If very young, such as 15 or less, they are unlikely to be skilled shooters, especially if they come from areas of the world where great unrest has been going on. No 15-year-old is likely to be a good shooter if they live today in Afghanistan or Africa. The skills it takes to develop good marksmanship have, no doubt, been denied to them. A 15-year-old in Switzerland or the US may be a trained shooter – but not in such areas as these. Your risk level goes down with the skill levels, obviously. If you see a bunch of middle- or old-aged men in the videos and see no glasses evident, you can easily conclude a lot of them are unable to see their sights properly due to eye degeneration. This is especially so in areas where eye diseases are so common no wise person will share binoculars with a native lest he become infected. If you cannot see properly, you cannot use your sights properly and thus will not be able to shoot efficiently.

Guerilla types in poor countries are unlikely to be equipped with body armor and helmets, but if you are looking at a formal army unit (like your allies perhaps), they at least should have such equipment if they are going to be "up to speed."

If you get an opportunity to see any "guerilla training films" of your opponents in their training camps, watch closely. Do you see ear plugs or muffs in evidence? No one can truly learn how to shoot properly without them. If you shoot enough rounds to become skilled, you will suffer constant ringing in your ears which will degrade your ability to hear at night. Do you see photos of them shooting bursts from their weapons or careful semi-fire? If bursts, they are unlikely to be truly dangerous. Remember also that certain types of groups, such as European terrorist groups, are unable to go shooting every couple of days to keep their hand and eye trained. The IRA for instance used to have to travel to Libya to shoot. I always feel bad about my 15-minute drive to the range and wish I could shoot out the back porch like my friend, Kent Lomont of Salmon, Idaho, does. No one who has to travel for a long time and gets infrequent range time will get and stay very good.

Do you see a lot of folding stock rifles in evidence? Naturally they are better for carrying under coats and, of course in non-urban areas, may have been what was available for capture but how do you see them shot? Folders frequently will wobble more than their fixed-stock brethren, although this is not always the case and they can be fixed after a fashion, but AKM folders especially are notorious for this fault. More critically, do you see them carrying (or worse shooting) them while folded? If so, you are obviously dealing with less skilled people as no serious person would utilize a rifle in that fashion. The person who shoots at you with a folded stock is extremely unlikely to hit you beyond close range.

If you can see the enemy shooting, what type of ammunition are they using? Do they use any tracer ammunition? Do they use all tracer ammunition? The better-skilled shooter will typically load the last few rounds in a magazine with tracer (especially with weapons lacking a bolt hold-open such as the Heckler & Koch G3 and AK series) then load two rounds of ball, then a round of tracer and so on to the top. Does your enemy? If they use ball, what type – real standard ball or AP ammunition? Steel-cored ammunition is obviously a lot better for penetration than conventional ball ammunition and will impose a greater risk to you and your equipment. Good AP ammunition will seriously effect helicopters to a much greater extent (and your body armor) than conventional ball. Does your enemy load his weapons with armor-piercing, including tracer, ammunition? If so, you may have some serious trouble ahead of you and you need to be guided accordingly.

Look at grenade use also. Do you see them in the photos? Of course, they may have simply thrust them into their pockets but most times, people with grenades seem to like to show them off. What type are they – defensive or offensive? Who made them? Some countries are well-known for poor quality control. How do they carry them as regards the pins? Have they removed the pins and placed a rubber band around the spoon and body as was common in ARVN (Army of the Republic of Vietnam) airborne and ranger units during the Vietnam War? Are the pins firmly flattened back on the body as they come from the factory, or have they been crimped somewhat more straight so they can be pulled out rapidly when needed, even if the soldier is weakened by wounds? Do they carry them in a position where they will fall off their gear during a night operation to be lost forever, or do they have them sufficiently secured so they can run and crawl across a field and still have them the next day? All will tell you how grenade savvy your opponent is likely to be.

Do you see a lot of females with grenades? Most lack the body strength and skill necessary to throw them far enough away not to endanger themselves, unless they can drop behind a solid object.

Do you see knives in any photos? How do they carry them? A field soldier does not need a knife too often for combat (although it has occurred more frequently than some might say) but a field soldier without a knife will find himself without a tool that can be used in a thousand commonplace fashions over time. Its lack will be sorely felt.

Do your opponents use RPG7s? If you see them in the photos with them, do you see the spare chest-mounted pouches holding spare grenades? If not, they are unlikely to pose a great risk to you in the long run.

While unlikely to be seen in photos from the Middle East, from Europe, Asia and Africa, we are occasionally greeted with film clips of "female warriors" chanting their normal dismal chorus of "Death to America, etc." While there is no reason why a female cannot shout as well as male, it is a rare female who is as strong as a male. In the US military, for instance, due to the influx of a large number of female soldiers to the field, duties which in years passed were considered to be one-man jobs have become two-person tasks. To be honest about it, artillery/mortar shells and boxes of ammo are heavy objects. Men are proportionally stronger than women in upper body strength in particular and thus able to handle these objects more readily. A unit which has females in it simply cannot be considered to be as effective as one with only men, all other factors such as training, intelligence and devotion being the same. Such a unit will require as much food and other support services as an all-male unit and yet will deliver a lesser result in all likelihood.

Other things to look for in your review of photos and similar sources is the presence (or absence) of first aid gear, canteens with water in them, small light packs holding such things as poncho liners, food for a day, spare socks, radio equipment, spare barrels for an LMG (without them, they are not nearly as effective – an M249 for instance without a spare barrel is not much better than an M16A2 and weighs more), general signs of preparation for night patrolling such as taped-down gear, painted metal finishes to avoid shine and generalized noise suppression efforts. Do you see maps and compasses evident, pencils and paper to write messages (not pens that freeze, leak and run in water so the message is lost in the rain)? Is your enemy prepared for a sudden change in weather? Do they have gloves or mittens to wear, good boots and something to keep the rain and snow away? Do you see any gas masks? If so, they can be using it against you. Smoke grenades in the photos?

If the radio is bad, smoke grenades can be a good alternative. Similarly, when you call in your location to airborne assistance whether a plane to bomb them or a helicopter to come take you away (or resupply you), you will no doubt "pop smoke" to guide them in. Do they have smoke to confuse the issue? Better look now and see. While they soon will from capture (and loss) you at least will get an idea about their capabilities.

Lastly, how long has it been since your enemy fought a well-trained foe? In Afghanistan for instance, the more senior men no doubt fought the Russians but most of the men in the field are unlikely to be old enough to have fought them. Thus you will be dealing with troops who are used to dealing with people equally skilled and equipped as themselves. Hopefully you are better. Among European terrorist groups, they are likely to be used to dealing with European police who must be charitably viewed as little better than government-paid watchmen. Over powering an unarmed constable or one armed with a hand gun and club only (coupled with poorly trained and little general aptitude) is a lot different than our overcoming a determined attack by a Special Operator who comes to the job with honed skills and good equipment.

Much can be learned from observing open sources of material about your enemy (and your allies). You just have to know enough to understand what you are observing and what it means. Hopefully this material here will prove to be useful in your education attempts.

Special Operations weapons

Chapter 6

While many people think of all sorts of exotic weapons when dealing with this issue, the first rule to remember is that special operations weapons frequently follow the rule for dances in the country – "you dance with the girl you bring." Simply put, a Special Operator, whether civilian or military, most frequently for a variety of reasons will be equipped with weapons that are the same as his less-trained colleagues and he must be able to perform the tasks assigned to him using these weapons using his experience and skill – not depend upon some exotic weapons or equipment which may very well not be available when the time of crisis develops or which may have been used up or destroyed in prior operations such that a re-supply in the face of over-stretched supply chains may simply not be feasible. This does not, of course, mean that there are not all sorts of unusual and exotic weapons that may prove useful for the Special Operator: it merely means he must always be prepared to perform his tasks with the most mundane of equipment also.

While there is quite a bit of crossover between civilian and military Special Operations weapons, the requirement is that military Special Operations teams performing military-type actions, as opposed to police-style work, use ammunition that complies with The Hague Convention of 1908 and also that is constantly in the supply chain, especially as their operations take more time and are located further from the home base of the team, and this imposes limitations on the Special Operations team. Additionally the need to maintain the weapons at the military level can be troubling if non-standard weapons are used. For instance, US Marine Corp. recon units at one time used the Heckler & Koch MP5 9 x 19 SMG. The weapons worked fine and 9 mm ammunition was in the supply chain, albeit being low-performance, full-metal-jacket, non-AP ball rounds. The Marines shot their weapons a lot and carried them a lot. As a consequence, like all good Marines, they broke them. Each time it happened, the weapons had to go back to the supplier to be fixed. Even when they had good spare parts so they could fix them "in–house," getting the spares was difficult and the manufacturer would not supply certain parts, demanding the weapons be sent back, ultimately to Germany in some cases, to be fixed. Obviously that put the team short of weapons for an extended time and, of course, it involved a lot of paperwork in authorizing the shipment, paying for it and making certain they got them back. It was too much ultimately and the Marines dumped their old beat-up MP5s (and parts) on to the FBI, adopting the M4A1 carbine for the teams instead. Ammo was more powerful, spares were readily available, and they could be repaired/re-supplied "in-house." So it is with lots of military Special Operations units. The ability to get ammunition, spare parts and repairs, plus ease of training with standard weapons, may well outweigh the possible performance increase to be had by using specialized weapons. Another factor that must be considered with Special Operations units at the military level is that the people who come to such units are not unnecessarily "gun people." They may really only know the weapons they are formally trained with at military schools. They are unlikely to bring experience with a wide variety of weapons obtained at their own expense both in terms of time and money to the field. Instead

45

they come from standard units to the Special Operations units, trained only on standard weapons. To then train them on exotic specialized weapons takes time and money that many units will decide is better spent on other training programs that will increase their ability to perform a mission rather than concentrating on a specialized exotic non-standard weapon. A friend of mine who formerly served in the Selous Scouts is a perfect example of this type. This man is a highly trained and experienced operator and has done hundreds of Special Operations in many hot spots. He is not a "gun person" however. He is familiar with the FN-FAL and the MP5 as these were his regular firearms. On a course one time, he had an UZI SMG and, forgetting for a moment it was an open-bolt gun, attempted to close the weapon by lowering the bolt on a loaded round like he would do with an MP5. Naturally it fired! Being an experienced man, no harm was done as it was pointed in a safe direction. This was strictly due to his unfamiliarity with the UZI SMG. So it is in every Special Operations unit in the world. Merely being in one does not mean you are interested in firearms. This is especially true in military units, oddly enough.

Additionally, in military units utilizing specialized non-standard weapons creates a training problem. The military trains from manuals. If they have no course of fire for the weapon, then it must be developed by someone who is familiar with the weapon and knows its strengths and weaknesses so a proper course of fire can be developed and individuals who are interested get the benefits of the strengths and minimize its weaknesses. In military units, in particular, with specialized non-standard weapons, it may simply not be possible to find someone to do this. Thus an outside expert must be brought in to teach the class and develop the range program. This is an extra expense many Special Operations units may wish to avoid, spending the money instead on other things that have a higher priority for mission accomplishment. Also the military facilities may simply not be set up to handle this special weapon and its ammunition, so again the benefits to be obtained by its use are outweighed by its cost. For instance when the US Marine Corp decided to adopt the MP5 for its Star War Defense Unit, no one was capable of teaching the class on it within the Marines and my friend, Evan Marshall (former Detroit Michigan SWAT man and homicide detective) was hired by Col. Young, the unit commander at the time, to do it. The new FN Five-seveN pistol may very well be difficult for a military Special Operations unit to utilize because of ammunition supply, parts, maintenance and the fact that military handgun ranges are not set up to handle this highly potent round.

Military Special Operations units also must deal with potentially greater numbers of enemies; they must be prepared for more dangerous opponents, such as tanks and planes and, of course, frequently will engage targets at a much greater distance than their civilian counterparts.

While all the above may make it seem that the civilian Special Operations units have a much easier time of it, they are faced with their own difficulties. First and foremost, civilian Special Operations groups always tend to face greater scrutiny than their military counterparts. While in military operations, some casualties are to be expected both in training and actual operations and non-combat injuries are to be avoided, they are not subjected to the potentially damaging lawsuits and indictments that follow such problems in a civilian Special Operations context.

The civilian Special Operator is unlikely to be involved in an action for an extended period of time and is unlikely to be engaging in an action involving the high number of individuals and hard targets such as tanks and planes as his Special Operation military counterpart, but the civilian Special Operator is held to a much higher standard as regards use and application of deadly force.

The civilian Special Operator frequently is a part-time operator being forced to do more mundane tasks most of the time, unlike high-end military teams that are dedicated to the subject. As a consequence of this split in activity, the civilian Special Operator often finds training times, especially training time as a unit, very difficult to obtain. They must thus spend the time wisely, using the available time for things that are important rather than "fun" or "daring." For example no civilian police team needs to learn how to "fast rope" (i.e., use a thick rope like a fireman's pole to deploy) from a helicopter in all likelihood. Better to spend the time practicing their sniper work or something similar.

On the flip side, the civilian Special Operator team can expect their personnel to come to the field with greater firearms experience over a wider range of weapons, so they may well be able to use more exotic mission enhancing weapons. Similarly ammunition re-supply, spare parts, and maintenance are substantially easier to manage than in a military team which has a bigger logistics tail and may well be stationed in areas where the UPS truck does not come every day.

In military Special Operations units, personnel are often selected for non-combat/non-gun handling skills and are armed more as an afterthought than anything else. For instance, a person may be a member of the team because of his unique language, communications or medical skills. In a civilian team, there is a much lesser need for these specialized skills and much more emphasis can be placed on weapon-handling skills. As a consequence, the civilian team members are very likely to be able to handle a much wider range of different weapons than their military counterparts. Additionally, since they will not need to learn how to handle certain weapons like heavy machine guns, rocket launchers, anti-armor weapons, the civilian teams can spend that time on mastering different rifles, shotguns, SMGs and handguns instead, thereby gaining greater proficiency with them.

Before going on to specific weapons found in Special Operations units and evaluating their good and bad points, one last point about the difference in weapons used and approach should be noted. Military teams will often deploy to areas where they wish to be deniable. As a consequence, they may be issued with captured enemy weapons or weapons that at least do not reflect their standard military issue weapons. That way, if lost, they do not come back to embarrass the country generally. This is the reason why specialized foreign weapons training can be crucial for military teams so they can become familiar with enemy weapons and World War II foreign weapons which still can be very effectively deployed in many situations. Obviously the civilian Special Operation teams operating domestically will not have any such concerns although they may well wish to use low-profile weapons that will not inflame already tense social issues or use weapons that will not appear to be extreme if seen in the local nightly news coverage. Hence they may wish to use weapons that alter the noise level or do not look like military weapons to help generally "soften" the image and avoid changes of the civilian Special Operator "militarizing police work."

Anti material/Anti-armor weapons

These are weapons designed to destroy equipment or armored vehicles. Obviously they have little value to civilian police teams although I suppose an occasion might arise where a police Special Operations team might want to destroy a generator or communication system without exposing officers to direct fire by their opponents and as such, these weapons could prove useful. Such occasions must be very few and far between. Even less likely would be the use of anti-armor weapons by fully civilian teams (although certainly some anti-armor capability might be in line for citizens in countries confronting police officials who wish to use tanks on them).

For military Special Operations teams, however, both of these groups of weapons can be very useful. Taking anti-armor weapons first, obviously a Special Operation team, may very well deploy in areas where they will be confronted by enemy armor. The ability to destroy such vehicles becomes critical. The RPG-7 is readily available and has proven itself capable of destroying the biggest vehicles (or at least stopping them) in the world. LAW rockets (the US-made man portable anti-armor launcher) as well as various recent portable anti-armor, man-held weapons also are quite useful. Besides being used against vehicles of all types, they can be effectively utilized against bunkers you encounter, and you can blow holes in buildings with them to permit you to enter or exit a building at points other than doors or windows which are likely to be covered by the enemy with machine guns in urban areas. While I suppose a police team could find such abilities helpful, other less drastic measures would seem more likely to be used.

Anti-material rifles typically are of a bore size in excess of 50 caliber. Typical ones used by US forces chamber the .50 Browning Machine Gun (BMG) cartridge while others seen in Europe chamber the 12.7 x 107 mm cartridge or even 14.5 x 114 mm which is truly twice the cartridge of a .50 BMG. While such weapons can be used for long range sniping against individual human targets, their better use seems to be in destroying items such as missile launchers, radar installations and aircraft on the ground. Again, it seems unlikely that a police team would ever need to do this type of thing, although I suppose I could come up with some type of legitimate situations when such actions would be proper and useful but it is a leap in reality to say it is likely to be a necessary tool in the civilian Special Operator's box.

Weapons for such purposes come in single shot, bolt-action, repeater and semi-auto mode. All are long, fairly heavy, ill-balanced and quite noisy. Thanks to the development of really efficient muzzle breaks, the recoil on the weapons is really no greater than that felt with a full power 12-gauge Magnum shotgun load found in a typical field weight shotgun. While not pleasant, it certainly is not impossible for anyone to handle it for a large number of shots. The muzzle blast seems to be the most punishing in fact, and the Special Operator should always carry muffs to wear while shooting it if he is to avoid being disoriented by the blast (not to mention loss of hearing ability). The semi-auto rifles in .50 BMG, like the Barrett so successfully used by US forces in the Gulf War, is likely to be the easiest to shoot but lacks the finest in accuracy. Good bolt actions using match grade ammunition utilizing center ground bullets can group 10 shots into 4½ inches at 1,000 yards; obviously, that means it is a long-range weapon of some potency, for a shooter can thus engage targets such as missiles and aircraft at 2,500 yards with a degree of certainty of hitting them and thereby disrupting their ability to function. When fired from such a distance, the Special Operator has little real exposure to return enemy action as long as he can fire a few shots then leave the area.

Besides rifles in .50 BMG, 12.7 and 14.5 mm, 20 mm cannons used as anti-material weapons are seen occasionally. While early in World War II, such 20 mm cannons were thought to be anti-armor weapons, development in armor so quickly took place that they no longer were a viable armor threat. They could still be effectively used on trucks and similar soft-skin targets. As the 20 mm round can deliver quite a potential load to the target of incendiary material or explosives obviously such weapons can be used effectively as anti-material weapons. Unfortunately, due to the US law which lists those weapons as "Destructive Devices" unlike a .50 caliber rifle or less, US civilian shooters who effectively turned the .50 BMG cartridge and weapon into an effective long-range tool have not been able to work on making the 20 mm weapons more accurate and dependable. Accordingly, little real use seems to exist long-term for such weapons, due to the lack of accuracy exhibited, the weight of the weapons and poor general handling encountered by shooters when firing the weapons.

Grenade launchers

Grenade launchers come in a variety of forms useful in Special Operations. They come mounted on tripods or vehicles and fire either semi-automatically or in bursts. It seems unlikely to me that such launchers would have much use for civilian teams, but I suppose if used with riot gases of various types or perhaps wooden pellets (commonly called "knee knockers" in certain circles), they would be useful in riot situations. For the Special Operations military team, such launchers are extremely useful as getting almost the same effect as a mortar without the trouble of setting one up. These launchers can be used on a ground mount which is really too heavy to carry on foot but more critically can be mounted on Humm Vees and similar vehicles, allowing the Special Operator to carry them long distances and really have a very effective weapon to inflict damages onto the enemy and, possibly more critically, to deprive an enemy of an opportunity to enter an area.

US launchers tend to be 40 mm, while Soviet and Chinese ones seem to be 30 mm. Obviously each has its good and weak points but both roughly

M203 grenade launcher fitted to the AR-15 A2 – the author's choice for an infantry weapon.

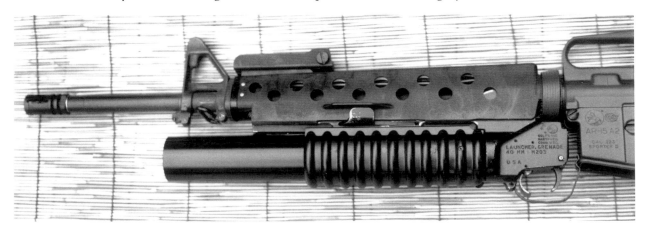

Special Operations: weapons & tactics

The author with the M79 40mm grenade launcher.

accomplish the same thing. The 40 mm launchers have a wide variety of munitions available to them such as high-explosive and gas as well as buckshot loads. I have not seen such a wide variety of loadings for the 30 mm weapons but, of course, they may exist and certainly could be developed if the need arose. The big problem with all such fused munition is the dud problem. If you fire a high-explosive round and it does not explode, it must be removed by an EOD (Explosive Ordnance Disposal) expert unless you are behind

Left-side view of the M79 40mm grenade launcher.

enemy lines and can leave it behind without concern. Obviously this represents a major problem for the civilian operator and likewise makes training with the rounds quite difficult as you must have a range where you can keep people totally out of the area even when not training lest they step on a dud and get hurt. Military ranges can do this but not civilian ranges typically.

Besides mounted grenade launchers, you have separate weapons dedicated to grenades like the M79 and launchers made a part of the rifle system such as the M203 attached to the M16 series of weapons. The M203 has also been modified to fit other weapons such as the AUG rifle and the H&K firm makes a launcher to fit a variety of military-patterned weapons. The Soviets also make a launcher they can mount on an AK 74 rifle which is handy. Interestingly enough, the Italians may have lead the way in this field with their separate grenade launchers which could be mounted below an M1891 TS short rifle in World War II.

Rounds of these launchers fall into the same patterns earlier discussed. For the military Special Operator, as with the standard infantryman, such launchers are incredibly useful, especially if mounted on a rifle so you are not down a rifleman to gain a grenade launcher. When I was in the service, at the beginning we had M79 grenade launchers and the grenade man carried it and a pistol (typically an M1911A1). This was a useful weapon but it did put your squad of 10 down two riflemen to gain it. If in a tight position where overhead cover prevented the firing of grenades, it typically looked like a poor choice. The M203, when it came in, was greeted with much enthusiasm as it got us two more riflemen while keeping our grenade men. The M203 was a bit harder to use effectively than an M79 but trained operators soon learned how to use it almost as well as the stand-alone M79. All the good things I could say about grenade launchers being used by standard infantry units applies even more so to military Special Operations units. The launchers will add some weight to the weapons which, of course, means the operator can carry less weight in ammunition (or something else) and, of course, the grenade munitions will similarly reduce cartridge ammunition loads but I believe the benefit of having the launcher and grenades will far outweigh the penalty incurred. I would go so far as to say that in Special Operations units, everyone not armed with a precision rifle or light machine gun ought to have an M203. I certainly prefer one on any rifle I take into hazardous conditions.

For the civilian police operators, an M203 or similar launcher can prove quite helpful also although the high-explosive rounds which are the standard military loads obviously will have little use. It's pretty hard to see how you can justify shooting a 40 mm, high-explosive grenade at a criminal subject much less a hostage scenario although I suppose I could come up with situations like the Texas Tower sniping event where it could prove helpful. For those who may not recall, this incident occurred in the early 1960s when a man got into the belltower on the campus of the University of Texas at Austin and, using the height of the Tower to his advantage, fired down on the passers-by for some period of time until a civilian and two police officers entered the Tower, shooting him at close range. Still, I am not certain I would want to take the political fall-out if I were the chief of a department, especially if it had missed and done some property, or worse, innocent-party damages. That being said, the launchers are very useful for blowing locks/hinges off and more typically firing gas into a location occupied by a subject. As in military teams, while special launchers could be used, having one attached to the rifle prevents you losing a rifleman to a gas gun.

Machineguns

Machineguns are like Goldilocks' porridge bowls – they come in three sizes and are for different purposes. A heavy machinegun is a weapon of 50 or greater bore size. A common model is the 50 Browning HB M2. This weapon is a tripod-mounted weapon weighing in around 150 pounds with all pieces and can be fired from a fixed position or from a vehicle. The DSLKM 12.7 is a weapon of similar power used by countries supplied by the old Soviet Union or China and fills the same role. These heavy machineguns can effectively turn the tide in battles and thus are great force multipliers. A military Special Operation team that wants to block the entry or exit of an opponent from an area may well find them very useful, especially if they have access to vehicles to move and carry the weapons and ammunition. Such weapons have a variety of special ammunition they use and since the bullets are large, they can

The author with a .50 caliber MZHB on a tripod.

Selous Scouts train here on a captured 12.7 mm enemy heavy machinegun.

hold quite a bit of explosive, tracer and/or incendiary ammunition material. With a heavy machinegun, you cannot destroy a tank but you can definitely destroy light-skinned vehicles at great range, building bunkers, installations of all types and enemy personnel. While a military Special Operations team which has access to vehicles should utilize them, it is hard to see what use they would have for a civilian special response team except possibly for maritime teams which may wish to stop a fleeing boat on the ocean. Even there, it seems quite dangerous to me to shoot a heavy machinegun into a boat and the

The author carrying a Heckler & Koch 21 LMG attached to a tripod which can be carried as a rucksack on the back.

The author with the Heckler
& Koch 21 LMG on a tripod
in the low mount position.

application of deadly force may prove to be excessive. That being said, I must say I personally know of a race riot that was stopped before it started in 1968 in a Missouri town by the presence of a 50 BMG M2 HG and 10,000 rounds along with an expressed willingness to rain rounds down on the potential riot zone. I gather the riot leaders were convinced the operators were crazy enough to use it and the rioting never materialized. Perhaps the technique would work today but I am doubtful and I rather think I would not want to put up with the lawsuits or federal civil rights investigations if I were the Chief.

Medium machineguns were originally defined as water-cooled, rifle cartridge-firing weapons that weighed over 30 pounds and were fired off a tripod. If we take this definition now, they are unlikely to be useful to either military or civilian Special Operation teams. Nowadays, some people would

The author with a PKM
7.62x54R LMG with a 100-
round box attached.

The author firing a PKM LMG from the shoulder point position.

view as medium machinegun a 30 caliber, full-power, rifle cartridge-firing machinegun as opposed to a light-weight machinegun that fires either .22 ammunition or sub-full-power 30 loadings. Among the first group are things like the MAG 58, M60, MG3 and H&K 21 to name some currently available products, and among the latter group are the RPD 7.62 x 39 mm, RPK and RPK-74 and M249 to name but a few of the current crop of LMGs. Things like the Bren, FN-D, BAR, ZB37 fire full-sized rifle cartridges but either take a detachable box magazine only or lack a quick change barrel. They are not suitable for long-term continuous fire although perfectly adequate for 300–400 rounds fired quickly which should take a person through many instances where a weapon will be needed.

As with standard infantry troops, these medium- and light-weight machine-

German troops firing the MG42 LMG from a tripod.

Special Operations: weapons & tactics

An MG34 on a Lafayette tripod being fired using a long-range sight.

guns are useful for the military Special Operator. They are, of course, force multipliers, as, especially with Special Operations troops, the machinegun will increase the ability of the few Special Operators who are working on their own often behind the lines or beyond the ability to call in supporting fires to deliver maximum fire on the enemy soldiers. Most current machineguns of these types are totally dependable although each has its own good and bad points. While these weapons can be used on vehicle mounts and off ground-mounted tripods, they are especially useful as they are light enough to be carried in the field on land-mobile operations. In such situations, they are typically used off a bipod which naturally does not give as much stability to the firing platform as a tripod, making bullet dispersion greater, but when

The author firing a Czech ZB26 LMG – note the case in the air.

The author with ZB26 8mm LMG

used in such roles, they are fired at closer distances also so the consequences are not too harmful. For the purpose of denying an enemy access to an area or long-term suppressive fire while other elements of the group attack a target, naturally the tripod should be utilized. Each of these air-cooled weapons, whether belt- or box-magazine-fed, should be accompanied by a spare barrel or two to permit the weapon to be used in the most effective fashion possible. Limiting such a machinegun to one barrel as occurred in Panama with US troops using the M249 is really to reduce the weapon to the status of a standard infantry rifle as the fire continuity which is one of critical features or the machinegun will be lost. Teams of soldiers, whether traditional or Special Operator, must know how to quickly get the weapon into operation and keep it in operation by altering the burst with supporting machineguns to avoid overheating and also know how quickly to exchange a hot barrel for a cool one at proper intervals.

In Special Operations units, such machineguns should certainly be issued at the identical levels found in traditional infantry units and possibly greater numbers should be used to get the extra multiplier effect so desirable in a special unit.

While the machinegun will play an essential role in the military Special Operations unit, it is rather difficult to see how such things can be utilized lawfully except on very rare occasions by the civilian Special Operation teams. I can think of some instances where it might be useful and justified but

The author with a PI (Product Improved) version of the M249 LMG. Note the new stock design and flat top to hold the Elcan scope or night sights. The weapon is fitted with a 200-round box magazine unit. A great weapon for special operations military teams but unlikely to be used by civilians.

apart from some very odd circumstances, it would seem to me that the civilian Special Operations team would be best advised to spend the money on buying and training with such weapons on other things.

Shotguns

The combat shotgun is rather the flip side of the machinegun. Both weapons are designed to throw patterns of projectiles (pellets in the case of the shotgun, bullets in the case of the machinegun) at a distance in the hopes of having one or more of them impact a target that is moving, indistinct, or otherwise

Photograph of British soldiers taken during Malaysian "Emergency Days" with (left) the Remington M870 shotgun and (right) the Bren LMG .303.

difficult to strike with a single projectile-launching weapon. In the case of the shotgun, it is designed to throw deadly patterns at as much as 60 yards (usually a lot shorter, say, 20 to 25 yards) and in the case of the machinegun, up to 1,100 meters (again, usually a lot shorter, say 300 to 500 yards). Because of these features, each weapon is better or worse for certain types of duties. As we have noted, the machinegun is an especially useful weapon for military Special Operations units and a poor one for the civilian Special Operations team. The exact opposite is true with the shotgun with it being an excellent weapon for the civilian Special Operator.

In many areas of the world, the shotgun has become a lot less popular with Special Operations units in recent years. Much of this is simply due to fashion, not the tactical concerns, although clearly there are occasions when a single surgical strike is called for at close range and if that ever occurs, a multiple projectile launching shotgun simply will not do. The old method was to simply transition to your handgun but, especially among military-based teams used for civil policing in some countries, unfamiliarity with handguns has caused them to flee to the SMG solution which has its own drawbacks as we shall see.

Combat shotguns come in all types of actions: single- and double-barrel, bolt-action, pump, lever and auto-loading. While there are occasions when a single- or double-barrel shotgun can come in very handy for Special Operations units (I remember an eight-inch double-barrel, 20-gauge shotgun being carried under a coat by a member of a famed Executive Protection Team while the principal worked the crowds), for the most part, apart from

Group shot at 20 yards with Federal Tactical 00 Buck in M1200 Winchester Trench guns; ex. Texas National Guard weapon from the late 1960s.

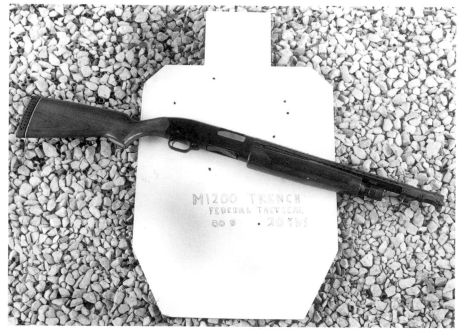

The author with M870 modified by Scattergun Tech. with a 14" barrel fitted.

The author testing the Bland 20 gauge Howdah pistol.

The author testing the Remington 11-87 Police shotgun – note that the fired case is still in the air yet the marksman is already back on target. Good sights and quick-firing, tactical loads give good control.

Special Operations: weapons & tactics

The author with the Valtro 12 gauge 13½" magazine-fed shotgun. possibly the best pump-action combat shotgun ever made to date.

using one as a speciality weapon to fire door-penetrating slugs then dropping it on the ground after use due to its low weapon potential, such weapons are best avoided. Bolt-action shotguns are generally longer and slower than is desirable but the recent advent of the fully-rifled, barreled, bolt-action shotgun coupled with a good scope and proper slugs certainly offers the potential for an excellent sniper field to the civilian Special Operator who only rarely will need to shoot beyond 100 yards. Such projectiles offer excellent stopping power and do offer the excellent prospect of a low-profile weapon for the aftermath of any police shooting but the slugs do penetrate a lot and

Winchester M12 riot gun as supplied to the US Military.

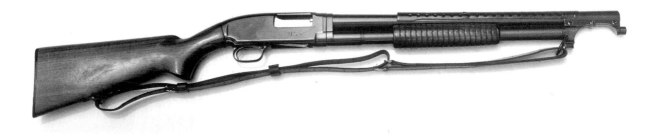

The author testing the Remington M870 Police Express 12 gauge shotgun.

US Navy SEAL deploys with the M870 Remington 12 gauge shotgun.

The author with the M97 Winchester riot gun, 12 gauge.

tend to bounce off hard objects so a light weight, high-speed, fragile projectile is generally thought to be a better alternative.

Occasionally lever-action shotguns are seen but for the most part, they have been obsolete for over 100 years and none should be seriously considered by any Special Operations team.

Pump-action and semi-automatic shotguns are the typical fighting shotguns we need to consider. Unfortunately whether for military or civilian teams, all the available shotguns save one style are merely modifications of commercial hunting shotguns. As such, they tend to be difficult to maintain, somewhat fragile, slow to load, have marginal safeties and poor sighting equipment. Why this should be is a mystery to me as you would think some sensible manufacturer would seize the opportunity to market a true fighting shotgun

Firing the M10B Hi-Standard autoloading shotgun. The sights are marginal and need to be improved; it should have been a 20 gauge weapon.

The author with a folding stock 20 gauge Saiga shotgun.

but none is built to a proper standard. The Russian Saiga is currently the best and even that could be improved.

A proper fighting shotgun should have a rapidly detachable magazine holding at least 8 to 10 rounds. It should have a positive safety, easy to engage and disengage. It should be totally reliable, have a barrel no longer than 12 inches, be finished with a highly rust-resistant finish, have excellent battle-style sights, be chambered for 20-gauge ammunition, and possibly utilize a folding stock so it can fit under clothing and in cars readily. Instead of such a purpose-built piece of kit, we get commercial weapons with no sights save a bead, a bead-blasted finish topped by a rough blue job, and a tubular magazine holding 4 to 7 rounds. The safety is generally small and difficult to work, and the design itself does not lock the action so the weapon can frequently fire, even with the safety on, if dropped or driven across enough tar strips.

The thing that really dooms the shotgun for the military Special Operation user is the limited capacity and slow reloading. My friend Leroy Thompson, who carried a Remington M870 while on Special Operation in Laos and Vietnam, acknowledges the difficulty of carrying spare ammunition and dropping shells in the mud as he attempted to reload. His only response to the statements that such things are unacceptable is to say he never, save once, needed to reload when he did not have plenty of time to do so. A lucky boy, my friend Leroy. The limited capacity, light penetration and slow reloading effectively remove the shotgun from any serious consideration as a Special Operations weapon, in my opinion. Almost any SMG will give you better results in such a military context and if you pick some of the better designs, they are not any heavier either. A lot easier to maintain in the field also. When our Special Operator crawled across no man's land in 1917 and the other alternatives were a long, heavy, automatic rifle or manually repeating rifle for shoulder-fired weapons the modified commercial pump or self-loading, 12-gauge might have made sense but not now. Button top shoes made sense also at one time but not now.

In the civilian Special Operations context, the limited penetration and lack of ability to carry extra ammo in any convenient fashion are not real drawbacks. Even the difficulty of maintaining the weapon is not a concern since no police weapon ever gets used on a continual basis like an infantry weapon. The low capacity is troubling but fortunately in our civilian situation, the number of shots fired in any event will be so few you are unlikely to empty your shotgun. Thus what we have today is not impossible to use although certainly it could be purpose-built and designed better. The major trouble seems to be the high recoil that such shotguns produce which can be troubling during extended training sessions. Before laughing at this, I will acknowledge being black and blue for five days once after teaching a combat shotgun class where I ended up shooting 250 rounds of high brass, 12-gauge buckshot through my Hi-Standard M10B shotgun. Using lower power "Tactical Loads" which, as they have a lower velocity and similar payload of pellets, recoil less is one solution, although it also lowers the overall range you can use your shotgun in to engage human targets by at least five yards or alternatively, and actually better, going to 20-gauge, which has all the power of the 12-gauge Tactical loads yet makes up a much more nimble or lively feeling weapon are solutions to this recoil problem. Of course, another solution is to embrace the "no pain – no gain" training motto. I tend to prefer that approach but also state that the preferred fighting shotgun should be similar to, but an improved version of, the 20-gauge Saiga.

For many uses in a civilian Special Operations team, a good fighting shotgun is hard to beat. A better fighting shotgun than the ones we have currently would even make it more useful and desirable rendering the current tendency to embrace the pistol-powered SMG in those same circles much less common. More the pity we do not have it now – but perhaps in the future?

Submachineguns (SMGs)

The SMG is an odd weapon in many aspects. It is a weapon that only existed in first string arsenals for a very brief period of time, starting in 1918 but really more like 1940 in many cases, and it continued to be used widely after it was already clearly obsolete due to the arrival of the .30 M1 carbine. It was removed for the most part by the mid-1960s, a very short lifetime. The SMG

The author with the Thompson M192/8 SMG the so-called Navy model, actually more commonly used in police agencies.

Special Operations: weapons & tactics

The author with a suppressed Sterling SMG. This is the military version L34A1.

Right side view of the Sterling L34A1 suppressed SMG.

basically suffers from a variety of limitations to the military user and most of those apply to your military Special Operator as well. They are heavy, inaccurate, take a special round of low-powered ammunition, and offer little to make up for these deficiencies. Of course, a lot of red-blooded American boys, having grown up watching John Wayne movies and "Combat" on TV, naturally want to pack a Thompson if they can. A few do and most of them, if sensible, immediately figure out that it is a poor choice. The only legitimate remaining use for the SMG by the military Special Operator today is used as

The author shooting the Walther MPK 9mm SMG.

a suppressed weapon. Due to the low power of the pistol cartridge used in the SMG, it is quite readily suppressed. Very excellent add-on suppressors as well as factory-built SMGs with suppressors like the H&K MP5 SD and Sterling MK VI exist and these weapons can prove very useful for our Special Operator who may need to shoot his weapon without alerting everyone in the area. The rushing water passing under a guarded bridge was sufficient to cover the low noise a suppressed Sterling MK VI gave out when a friend of mine once shot the bridge guard in the head at 100 yards. He then could set the charges and blow the bridge, tying up traffic for several weeks at that point. So useful are these weapons I would certainly say any Special Operations team would be remiss if they failed to include at least a few in their bag of tricks. Unfortunately if you deploy with one, you have thus taken one operator out of the fight generally speaking as he will not be able to carry his suppressed SMG and a standard weapon; he thus will be carrying a low-powered weapon using a special cartridge, thereby limiting his ability to engage the enemy. This is a real limitation taken against the prospect of a supposed possible benefit of using the weapon under unusual circumstances. Still, if you anticipate the need to approach guarded facilities, it can be very useful and far easier to utilize effectively than a suppressed pistol.

As with so many aspects of weaponcraft in Special Operations, the exact opposite analysis occurs when we go to civilian Special Operations situations. There the low penetration of the pistol-powered SMG and short range are not major handicaps as the ranges involved are short and concern for over-penetration with attendant risk to innocents is a great concern. The fact that a different cartridge is inserted in the inventory chain is not critical as the number involved will be small and re-supply as easy as going back to a vehicle as close as a few hundred feet away in most instances.

One of the biggest problems facing civilian Special Operation teams is that as they deal in urban areas, any gunfire noise associated with their activities is

The author just finishing a two-shot burst (note the two empties in the photograph) with a Colt 9mm, a closed-bolt SMG.

likely to bring unwarranted attention to them and possibly create urban strife or riots. As the military operator can use the suppressed SMG to good effect, so also the civilian Special Operator will find the suppressed SMG an excellent tool. In the military context, the burst-fire capability of the SMG is very useful for dealing with indistinct targets especially at night for a burst of rounds will cover an area, hopefully with at least one round hitting the target. The civilian Special Operator will not need this feature as he must make certain of his target and be able to hit it with each round fired lest he impose an unwanted danger on the community. A properly trained civilian operator can utilize fast semi-automatic fire to achieve the goal of rapid repeat strikes on the target to make up for the low power found in such pistol-cartridge-firing weapons without endangering the community.

Most SMGs which have been made in the last 50 years came with a provision for both semi- and full-auto fire. Most SMGs also fire from an open bolt position, firing the cartridge with the advance prime ignition principle that actually fires the cartridge before the bolt is fully forward but has the bolt going forward after the trigger is pulled. Many people, if not properly trained, find such open-bolt weapons more difficult to shoot well than closed-bolt models, although certainly this should not concern a Special Operations team which by definition is better trained. On the other hand, most available closed-bolt-firing SMGs are much more involved in their design so maintaining them is more difficult that most open-bolt designs. For our civilian team where conditions are much less rigorous, the maintenance problems are a minor issue whereas in a military environment, they are a critical issue especially as we go to maritime-type operations with a constant salt water and spray issue presented.

For our civilian Special Operation team using the SMG, the closed-bolt semi-automatic fire variant of the tested SMG design is probably best. You get the advantages of a tested design and are effectively arming your officers with a short-barreled, auto-loading carbine shooting a low penetrating load if you utilize the proper ammunition and can suppress it to avoid noise and the civil confrontations it can bring, while at the same time in the aftermath of news reports and lawsuits, the inflammatory "shot by an SMG-wielding policeman" issue is replaced with the officer firing surgically accurate strikes from his "pistol-powered carbine." This may not do any good, of course, but certainly can do no harm and the civilian Special Operator already realistically gives up nothing to get a tactical advantage in an incident and any time you can get a potential good thing while giving up nothing, it seems like a pretty good swap to me.

Rifles

The rifle is the standard weapon of both standard military forces as well as military Special Operations units. Rifles, for our purposes, break down into two basic classes with a couple of subclasses therein.

The first class is the precision rifle, commonly called the sniper's rifle. Typically these are bolt-action rifles (but not always), chambered for full-

Rare photograph of a World War I period US sniper with an M1903 wearing "gilly suit'.

powered rifle cartridges (but not always) and equipped with telescopic sights that typically include magnification beyond 3 or 4 X (but again not always). These rifles are typically used to shoot at selected human targets of importance. In the military environment, long-range shots in excess of 200 yards are the norm and typically in excess of 400 yards but despite lots of good stories about super long-range work, rarely beyond 800 yards. In the military Special Operations environment, they can be used to take out selected targets at long range, keep the enemy from operating against you without reservation by virtue of keeping them busy hiding rather than openly operating against you, and can be used to take out enemy positions at long range with surgical hits rather than frontal assaults which are often so costly. The military sniper typically does not care whether he kills his enemy immediately, a few minutes pause will not typically be critical, although the Special Operator frequently will want a more definitive death, although nothing like that imposed on his civilian Special Operations colleague.

Rifles that fall into this class of weapon include the various Remington M700-based rifles like the M40A1, the Accuracy International L96A1, French MAS36-based precision rifles and Heckler & Koch G3-based precision rifles. Older items such as the M70 Winchester and Enfield No. 4-based rifles are also occasionally seen in the field to this day doing yeoman work.

Of course, not everyone can utilize such a rifle and the person who is assigned this rifle must be trained to both safely handle and maintain it and also to master the skills necessary to bring out the potential of the weapon. This is done by selecting someone who is capable of understanding the ballistic issues (and mathematics) presented as well as someone who is both a trained marksman and who is willing to take individually selected shots on human beings.

A 3-shot group, shot at 100 yards by the author using the Pattern 1914 "T" rifle. Not too bad for a rifle and scope that was almost 80 years old on the day this group was shot (August 1994).

The author with a Czech 254 7.62 x 54R mm sniper rifle.

Military-environment rifles generally require a higher level of long-range accuracy than those used by the civilian operator who typically will not shoot beyond 100 yards. The civilian operator can use greater care in transporting and maintaining his weapon so he does not need to be as concerned about damaging his weapon or rendering it useless. A short barrel can be just as accurate as a long one and a well-designed stock and light barrel equally as

Top: Left side view of the Heckler & Koch STG-1 sniper unit –
the only H&K with a good trigger in the author's experience,
but the locking system still produces higher recoil levels.

Below: The author with the
Enfield L42A1 7.62 x 51mm
sniper rifle.

Right side of the L42A1 Enfield rifle with a 3-shot group shot at 100 yards using 168gr. Federal ammo.

Below: M1 Garand sniper rifle, left side. Note the scope mount with levers to allow removal.

Special Operations: weapons & tactics

The author with Accuracy International AWP 7.62 x 51 mm rifle with a Schmidt & Bender telescopic sight.

Full-length right-side view of an Accuracy International PM sniper rifle, 7.62 x 51mm NATO. This is a long, heavy rifle but it shoots well.

Group shot at 560 yards prone by the author using a Steyr Tactical Scout 308 equipped with a Schmidt & Bender 1.5 x 4 scope and Black Hills 168 gr. match ammo.

accurate at least for the few rounds our sniper is likely to shoot at one time. Certainly heavy barrels heat up more slowly and for long strings fired at the range, the heavy barrel may be superior, but if a sniper fires more than three shots from one position without a long time between the third and fourth shots, I believe he is way too optimistic about survival. Rifles suitable for high-country sheep-hunting carried by men in their 40s and 50s (dare I hope 60s?) make much better sense to me than some of the monsters we see on this stage from time to time.

Special Operations: weapons & tactics

The author with an AR15 rifle with a Colt scope, collapsible butt and FAKTS suppressor.

The civilian Special Operator may wish to include specialized features such as folding stocks to permit readily concealing the rifle from the news cameras as the target is approached and suppressors to help moderate the muzzle blast and subsequent neighborhood disturbance. Excepting odd special military operations where the team is going into an area to remove a dedicated human target and then will be removing itself from the area, such items are probably unnecessary for the military team. If they are, however, charged with such tasks, then they may prove quite helpful.

The biggest issue with the precision rifle at either the civilian or military level is acquiring the proper ammunition for it. In the civil context, this is easy to arrange and the number of rounds fired and availability to readily re-supply is so easy the matter need not concern anyone. It is rather like in deer hunting – a box of 20 will actually last, in all likelihood, for a decade of actual shooting. In the military context, this is not so as many more occasions may arise to fire the weapon and re-supply can be difficult due to supply channel problems. The military Special Operator must obtain a large stockpile of the proper ammunition and keep it readily available if he is to be useful. A precision rifle will be chambered for the typical machinegun round readily available in the unit, but loaded with such standard ammunition it will be little better than a slow-firing standard infantry rifle and the benefits of the precision rifle are effectively taken away. Weapons of all types are after all mere projectile launchers.

In years within the memory of many who will read this, the standard infantry rifle could be a manual repeater or a self-loading rifle. I think it fair to state that today and for the future, it is unlikely to be anything other than a self-loader. It, of course, may be a semi-auto only or a selective fire rifle. The military Special Operator, due to concerns of training, maintenance and re-supply, is unlikely to use anything other than the typical military infantry rifle of his country unless it is either a minor variant or the country involved is substantially behind on the developmental curve in such matters. Of course, occasionally Special Operations personnel will pick up a special rifle for their unit, more to make them different than for any real tactical reason, and such things are viewed by those in the know with amusement. Occasionally the standard infantry rifle has been selected and maintained due more to political considerations rather than weapon excellence and when this happens, the Special Operation military unit can often get away from such things that are foisted on to the general military and they will select a different weapon also. This is what has happened in England where the SAS/SBS has managed to avoid deploying the L85A1 rifle.

The civilian Special Operations team, of course, will not be concerned about weapon maintenance and re-supply like the military man. Nor will they be concerned about familiarity except marginally as they will train their members from the ground up, although obviously many ex-military types gravitate to law enforcement and hence to civilian Special Operation teams. Similarly, many "gun people" go into law enforcement and Special Operations, so a weapon that is familiar to such people being used by the police team could certainly not be harmful although obviously a "gun person" will be able to quickly become familiar and capable of using any selected weapon.

But the fact that the civilian team is not linked to a standard military rifle does free them considerably, permitting them to possibly select a better weapon for their unique needs and situations. As most civilian Special Operations will be over rapidly (in comparison to military operations) and will take place in urban areas where innocents are present, short rifles shooting ammunition unlikely to excessively penetrate a target, and that can be shot rapidly but accurately, are most desirable. Semi-auto rifles will

Left side of a FAMAS 5.56 x 45 mm rifle.

Top: Right side view of
FA MAS 5.56 x 45 mm rifle.

Below: Comparison of the
sizes of the Colt M16A2
(AR15A2) (top) and the
FA MAS rifle (below).

Current Bullpup 5.56 x 45mm rifles in use: top, the Steyr AUG, center the FAMAS and below, L85A1 with Susat scope sight.

accomplish everything necessary for a police Special Operation team, but I think the shorter barrel variants from 12 to 16 inches are better overall. While many offer excellent peep-sight systems, I believe some type of optical sight such as is found on the AUG, the ACOG (Advanced Combat Optical Gunsight), or Elcan will make for a better overall performance package. Military rifles are of known reliability and the semi-only variants of the M16 / M4, SIG 552/1, H&K G36, 33, and 53, M4A1, Galil and FAMAS all make excellent civilian Special Operations weapons when utilized with proper ammunition. Soviet pattern rifles such as the AKSU in 5.45 x 39 mm are also quite good, far superior to any SMG shooting a pistol cartridge. Standard model AKM rifles are not bad either although care must be taken to select the proper ammunition to minimize over-penetration. The sights are not too good on such rifles, however, and thus they fall well below the standard of any of the earlier mentioned rifles when equipped with an optical sight unit of the type mentioned earlier. Unfortunately there is no good, easy way to mount such sights on an AK-pattern rifle, that makes a handy package in my

Special Operations: weapons & tactics

Left-hand view of an M4 carbine (this one is the AR15A2 semi carbine) mounted with an Elcan scope – an excellent unit/combo.

The author with L1A1 fitted with L2A1 Susat sight.

opinion. The present side mounts on the receiver make the scope too high and leave the shooter's face unsupported by the stock.

Another weapon that is not seen too frequently today but was quite common in the 1960s is the US M1 Carbine. It is also an excellent choice for the civilian Special Operations team offering a light-weight small package with good accuracy and excellent stopping power when proper ammunition is used. Fashion more than intelligent weapon analysis has caused it to be seen infrequently today which is truly a shame as it is quite good. Additionally it is a very low-profile weapon which sometimes can be a major concern for agencies. A good modification of the weapon making it even more handy is to cut down the barrel about six inches; it takes very little away from the weapon except possibly 25 yards of effective range. For police operations, it still is more than adequate out to 200 yards which is well beyond what typically will be required of the Special Operations team.

Handguns

For most military and police organizations, the handgun is actually merely a badge of office. It is rarely if ever actually used and, especially in the military, is typically not considered a very important weapon. For the Special Operations team members, however, this is not the case. The handgun can be a very important part of the Special Operator's kit.

Many military teams in the US seem to utilize modified M1911A1 .45 ACP pistols. I believe this is because of the impact of Col. Jeff Cooper and his followers on such special units. Many of the people who are members of these units have been trained at places where Col. Cooper's influence is quite strong or in some cases they have even been trained at Gunsite in Arizona, the Colonel's training center. His training program and the course of fire they shoot rewards emphasis on the single action .45 caliber pistol. As a consequence, some military Special Operations people have apparently gotten a mission confused with a match. The special expeditionary recon Marine unit, for example, has modified M1911A1 pistols to get a weapon that really would make a very nice ISPC match gun but is not really suitable for a military Special Operations team.

As with typical infantry units, the pistol in a Special Operations unit should only be used in the event the main weapon goes down. Accordingly it should be small and light-weight so you do not lose rifle ammunition or grenades to a seldom-used pistol. In the military context, it also must use ammunition acceptable to The Hague Convention and should be capable of penetrating ballistic vests that are more and more commonly encountered in the military field or pouches full of steel magazines filled with steel-cased ammunition. Standard .45 ACP ammunition simply will not cut it when confronted with such tasks. Handguns that weigh 39 ounces (empty and are so big that they must be carried on the belt taking up space better filled by a spare magazine pouch holding 90 extra rifle rounds, a grenade or possibly (and even more useful) a canteen of water) seem excessive to me – and I like .45 Government Model pistols. The Special Operations military handgun should be light, small and a vest penetrator. This in addition to the other typical requirements of dependability, safety and ease of shooting. Good examples of such weapons are the S&W M940 and 9M both of which will accept 9 mm AP loads and yet can be carried in the top pocket of a fatigue shirt easily. One would suppose other weapons might prove useful also if proper ammunition was obtained like a PM (Makarov) with AP ammo, various .38 small-size revolvers or auto-loader chambered for the newly developed FN Five-seveN x 28 mm cartridge if made into a small, handy piece. The current FN Five-seveN pistol is light enough but is as big as an M1911A1 pistol so you gain some weight saving by using it but nothing else.

Of course, there may be times when military Special Operations teams will use a handgun as their primary tool. An example might be some type of raid or snatch group where one or more people may find it difficult to use anything other than a handgun. When this occurs, then a more traditional-size handgun is called for, like the FN Five-seveN which gives high capacity AP penetrating capability and good stopping power. Even in these situations, the current response seen, especially in the US, of adopting M1911A1 .45 ACP-type pistols is wrong as it lacks the ability to penetrate ballistic vests or the variety of field gear confronted today.

Civilian Special Operation teams also use their handguns only as back up typically, although they may legitimately find more use for the handgun than their military counterparts. Members of such teams may well deploy in civilian clothes before a raid and find it impossible to carry shoulder-fired weapons as they do so. The hidden handgun, which can be instantly deployed, is the obvious answer. Similarly the first man who enters a room or the man using the body bunker should be armed with handguns. I say handguns in the plural as obviously any such team member should carry two identical main battle pistols, one in his hand and the other instantly available should the primary piece run dry, be disabled by hostile fire or malfunction. In any case, it can be dropped and the second weapon instantly pulled as its replacement.

The civilian operator also will not need to carry as much equipment on his belt and thus can afford to give greater space for a handgun on his belt. This typically will be the handgun that is carried when not deployed for a raid. Accordingly the civilian Special Operator's handgun can be bigger and heavier than his military counterpart. Unlike the military operator, the civilian Special Operators typically will not be facing armored subjects nor opponents draped with spare magazine pouches of ammunition. He will be very concerned about over-penetration and also instantly stopping the aggressive acts of his opponents. These concerns as well as the prototypical civilian hostage team shot of "a head shot on a terrorist who is holding a hostage near to them while pointing a gun or holding knife to the throat of the victim or a bomb switch in hand," causes the civilian operator to typically select weapons which are the easiest to shoot accurately and fast. This is in counterdistinction to the typical law enforcement agent's situation where often we saddle them with weapons that are more difficult to fire accidentally (and thus also harder to shoot accurately), as we do not want them to accidentally or unnecessarily shoot someone. The civilian Special Operator is expected to be better trained than his less-skilled associates on the beat and goes into a situation typically anticipating a shot. This Special Operator will typically be shooting an assailant to stop a life-endangering action involving a third person and only rarely be defending himself, while the standard officer will often be shooting to defend his own life. As we anticipate there will be innocent third parties present, we anticipate a life-saving (and taking) shot being fired in close proximity to those innocents and we try to make it easy to get the best

Two Glocks carried in the proper way: primary gun in cross-draw, secondary weapon on right hip to be available immediately in the event that the primary weapon is disabled.

The author with a test target shot at 5 yards with a Glock 18 on full auto. Note – no hits on hostage!

possible results. As all shooters know, the single most important thing to assist in getting good results on target is a good trigger pull. We thus accept the potential accidental discharge problem found in single-action trigger systems to give our civilian Special Operator this extra ability. Freed from the constraints of The Hague Convention and further unlikely to encounter armored subjects, the civilian Special Operator will typically adopt the best possible expanding ammunition to accomplish his dual tasks of instant incapacitation and low penetration. While studies have shown that very few rounds will be fired in any real-world operation, the ability of semi-automatic pistols of proven reliability with excellent trigger pulls commonly, although not always, causes these teams to select the semi-automatic pistol. Some teams, however, still use revolvers due to their greater stopping power and ease of shooting as well, I believe, to the certain flair they give the unit. The French GIGN are a perfect example of this with their MR 73 revolvers. Others like the FBI National Hostage Rescue Unit have gone to the wide body (14 shot) Paraordnance copy of the M1911A1 pistol while giving their local teams the same weapon design with a single-stack magazine. Others select weapons that may be in use by patrol officers but utilize the lighter trigger pull variant. This is common with the Glock which has such an easily-changed trigger pull, varying readily between 3.5 pounds to 11 pounds.

Some units will equip their members (or at least the members at the sharpest end of the stick) with machine pistols. Truly the machine pistol is

Opposite above: Right-side view of Star MD 9 x 23mm machine pistol – selector in full auto position.

Opposite below: The author with a test target shot at 5 yards with a Stechkin machine pistol with stock attached. Two shot bursts, first shot centered, second shot higher and right.

Ex-Soviet Stechkin machine pistol with stock fitted.

Beretta M93R with butt stock fitted.

The author with burst fire Heckler & Koch VP70 machine pistol. Note 3-shot burst pattern on target shot at 5 yards off-hand.

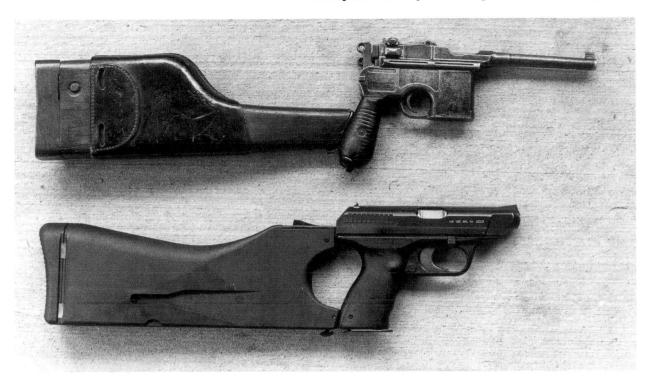

likely to be the single most effective anti-personnel weapon in the world at distances of up to five yards. Weapons, such as the Glock 18, Stechkin, H&K VP 70, Beretta M93 R and Star MD/PD can be truly devastating when used by the first man in the door on raids. But the person who is assigned those tasks and armed in that fashion must keep in constant practice to maintain the all too perishable weapon skills necessary to dominate the machine pistol. My experience tells me that anything less than 1,000 rounds of proper practice each month will simply not suffice to achieve the goal. Unless the team member is both willing and capable of this level of devotion to the task, he is better off with a standard handgun which will not be quite so effective but not so difficult to control.

Special Operations personnel are by definition people who will be assigned tasks where it is very likely that highly concentrated periods of violence will

Above: Right-side view of the Mauser M96 .30 Broomhandle with stock (top) compared to the Heckler & Koch VP70 9x19 mm (below). These weapons have a lot in common, despite major changes in construction and almost a century in time between them.

Below: Right-side view of the Heckler & Koch VP70 machine pistol.

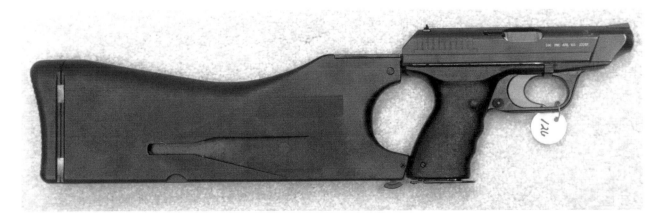

need to be dispensed. Of course, sometimes no shots will be fired and the mission, whether military or civilian, will take place without even a single round being fired. But no one who goes into a Special Operations unit should think for a minute that this will be the case. Instead they should figure they will need to fire their weapons accurately and quickly if they wish to come home. If they are unwilling or incapable of doing this, they should find a different position in the chain of command as ultimately the Special Operator is a sophisticated weapons user and this needs to be acknowledged at all levels. Their weapon selection (and training) thus are most critical for the accomplishment of their mission.

Opposite: Glock G18: top, right-side view with selector in the semi-fire position, below, left-side view with the selector in the burst fire position.

Chapter 7

Maritime operations & special weapons

Many Special Operations involve action around water to one degree or another. While there are works which detail training and equipment programs designed specifically for maritime Special Operations-oriented units, a few words should be included in a work of this type.

First it must be clearly understood that, while firearms are typically kept as dry as possible, it is really more for maintaining the finish on the weapon than it is for functioning. Most firearms will work fine whether exposed to fresh or salt water. The major functioning problem arises when they are exposed to the "surf zone" – that is the area between where you are in the water and getting out of it. There, as all who have even splashed about on the seashore with their children know, the sand is swirling about and will soon fill any nook or cranny. This means that the weapons must be either designed to provide plenty of leeway for such obstructions and also be capable of functioning in an unlubricated state for the salt water will soon remove most lubricants, or the weapon must be protected from the elements in some type of waterproof container. Obviously any weapon in a waterproof container renders it effectively useless as a weapon for the operator as he moves over the beach area but one assumes in that situation the operator will have a second weapon to defend himself as he exits the water and is finally in a position to safely open his waterproof container.

Some weapons, of course, are better for using in environments where

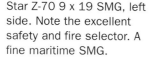

Star Z-70 9 x 19 SMG, left side. Note the excellent safety and fire selector. A fine maritime SMG.

The MAT 49 SMG with the stock extended.

they are likely to be penetrated by foreign subject matter than others. For instance, the MP5 is a finely fitted weapon which is certainly easy to shoot and accurate to within the limits of the ammunition. It is difficult to easily clean properly, however, and somewhat maintenance intensive as well as being fitted to a level that is more refined than other SMGs. For operations in the surf zone, even teams that typically use the MP5, have found other open-bolt SMGs, such as the Star Z63/70, MAT49 and UZI, are much superior as they utilize an open-bolt design which can withstand the sandy salt water environment better.

Most military pattern auto-loaders are also better in such environments than more finely fitted and difficult-to-maintain revolvers. While some fine military self-loaders like the SIG P210 would not be a good choice, typically rough-fitted Colt Government Models, Beretta M9/10, SIG P226/8 and, of course, Glock 17 pistols work exceptionally well. The tolerances are good and they are easily (more or less anyway – the Beretta has some oddities like the washers under the grips, the SIG the removal of the block in the receiver group and spring set-up and the Glock which is simply wonderful) cleaned.

Telescopic rifles are probably best left in the sealed containers although obviously scopes should be tested for sealing ability at depth if the operator will be swimming anywhere other than right near the surface.

Thanks to the off-shore oil-drilling industry and the space program, many very fine, highly rust-resistant finishes have been developed over the last 30 years, so if an operator is going to be involved with waterborne operations, I believe it is only sensible to have such a finish applied to help maintain the weapon, although as earlier noted, the weapons will work fine even in a salt-water environment in a standard blue configuration, they are simply much harder to maintain later. Finishes like Tennifer on Glocks, Brunitin on Berettas, Mellonite on Smith & Wessons, as well as commercially applied finishes like NP3, Black T and others are well known to many and can often seen among higher-end teams commercially applied to weapons that come factory-equipped with a standard blue finish. The only thing I would point

Right-side view of a Beretta M9, a standard military handgun found in some units.

out is that some after-market finishes will alter dimensions sufficiently to affect fitting. A thorough test to determine functioning should be carried out. Some are difficult to get applied also since shipping your fully automatic weapon to those who apply the finish may not be feasible due to legal entanglements.

Even with such finishes applied, a waterproof muzzle cap should be applied to the weapon (it's not a bad idea for all weapons carried in the field anyway, to keep water from the bore). Of course, such caps are not always available but in those situations, they can be taped over. With some weapons, especially handguns, this will not be possible, but if you can do so, there is no reason not to. Naturally they do not need to be removed when you are ready to shoot – you merely shoot through them assuming, of course, that they are plastic or rubber and not the brass types seen occasionally before World War II.

Once you exit the water and have an opportunity to clean you weapon if around salt water, the first step is to wash it thoroughly with fresh water to remove the salt. Then a standard, complete cleaning job is next. An air compressor to blow out the sand that seems to get everywhere is a great help. If properly maintained and especially if equipped with a good finish to begin with, there is no reason that the weapons should not look good and operate perfectly for years to come. In the Hemingway book *To Have and Have Not*, the main character placed his Winchester 30/30 and 12-gauge shotgun in sheepskin case lined with fleece that was constantly oiled to keep them from rusting on his boat in the Caribbean. Today we can do a lot better for a few years of that treatment will certainly lead to rusty bores and browned/red finishes.

When dealing with waterborne operations, the questions always come up about whether you can fire the weapon under water safely. The common myth is, of course, that they will blow up. The answer of course is "No" as long as the bore is full of water. If half full and especially if a small size like a .22, there may be bulged barrels but really no explosion. Some weapons have been designed or modified specifically to shoot underwater. The firing pin-cup modification to the Glock 17 is perhaps the one most commonly encountered with such cups to avoid water squirting back and tying up the firing pin. The Glock 17, as long as loaded with full-jacketed ammunition, will fire with perfect safety and reliability under water. Naturally the power level of the cartridge fired will be severely restricted as it is pushing through the water medium, but it will still hit a disabling blow at five to seven yards. Noise level is transmitted by water and can be a problem but, of course, if you need to shoot your weapon underwater, you likely have a bigger problem confronting you than the one that will follow after that problem is solved.

Any operator who will use his weapon around water (or for that matter in a high-humidity environment) should also test to make certain the ammunition is water resistant. Most commercially available ammunition is somewhat so but not to a level that will permit you to use it with confidence when exposed to long periods of insertion. The best way to do it is to order your ammunition directly from the factory demanding it meet waterproof specifications. The French GIGN team did this with their .357 Magnum ammunition made by Norma in Sweden. Naturally it is more expensive, but I suppose they believe it worth the cost. Of course, if you are in a position to do that, you might as well order it for muzzle-flash limits also as that is a really big problem in every case whereas water resistance is only a minor problem.

For those not capable of ordering the ammunition, test it by dumping it in water of the type you will operate in and see whether it will work for a period of time that you anticipate your operations will take. Then double it for safety. If the ammo won't work, dump it and get something else. If it will, then keep the ammunition you exposed in training segregated from the duty ammo. Shoot up in training any ammo exposed to the wet and watch your lot numbers. As you change lots, test them again to make certain the new lot of ammo is as good as the last lot.

Lanyards and slings are especially useful for maritime operations where the consequences of dropping your weapon can be a weapon lost forever. On the other hand, a lanyard or sling that gets tied up in something and will not break readily will carry you to the bottom of the ocean. Just such a thing almost happened to a Recon Marine a while back when the helicopter they were using to deploy to a ship got caught up in the ship and crashed into the ocean. As the Marine got out of the downed helicopter, his lanyard holding his Government Model .45 pistol snagged on the skids and began dragging him down with the chopper. Fortunately it ultimately broke and allowed him to swim to the surface but it was a near thing. A similar thing happened to a friend of mine once on a snow mobile and the lanyard got caught between a tree limb as he passed and the result was that he was literally pulled off the snow mobile. Lanyard and slings that can affixed a shoulder weapon to the shooter should be sufficiently strong to allow weapon retrieval but designed to break above a few hundred pounds in pressure. Such units are available. Do not simply tie the weapon to you with a web sling or parachute cord. It is shocking how strong such things can be when you do not want strength.

If your handgun or shoulder-fired weapon is equipped with a white light (or any other kind actually) source naturally it should be tested for water resistance and pressure under water. You then will need to modify or replace the unit as necessary or learn to live without it.

Maritime operations, whether actually in the water or merely around water, are important in the Special Operations world. Careful thought and preparation of the equipment that can be used for such activity will yield better results than would otherwise be the case and may in certain situations permit the operator to accomplish tasks that otherwise might well prove impossible. While much of maritime operations are the same as any other Special Operations, there are enough unique features and concerns to such operations that anyone who has the duty of equipping or training a unit whose duty will take them to such places would be wise to be alert to topics mentioned earlier.

Sniping in Special Operations – police v. military

A sniper in Special Operations is both a trained observer as well as someone who can hit small targets upon command. The skills of a sniper/observer are in demand for both police and military special observations, but the role they play is different, as are the ways in which they carry out their duties. Accordingly the equipment utilized and training they need to accomplish these differing jobs is not the same. Unfortunately all too frequently people confuse the roles and burden on the individual sniper with poor equipment and worse training.

A sniper in the law enforcement field is unlikely to ever shoot beyond 100 yards. In fact, 68 yards seems to be the typical average, as reported by the Federal Bureau of Investigation and municipal police agencies. The law-enforcement sniper must typically hit very small targets that will cause the party struck to immediately cease his or her actions. Only a brain shot or spine shot seems to be capable of delivering such instantaneous stopping. Thus very small targets at fairly close range are the norm for the police Special Operator.

The police sniper will typically be operating in urban areas and frequently be firing at high or low angles to the target. They must be familiar with such special shooting techniques. The urban sniper must always be concerned about being able to justify his shot in the event of criminal prosecution and, even more likely, civilian lawsuits filed possibly years after the incident when memories have become stale and the urgency of the moment is gone.

Another critical concern of the urban police sniper is dealing with potential riots caused by his shot. Thus the lower the profile presented both in physical appearance and noise level, the better for the police sniper. A sound sup-

3-shot group fired by the author at 100 yards with the Accuracy International sniper rifle from rest using 168 gr. SP Federal Premium ammunition.

pressor becomes a quite handy object thus being well worth the time and expense involved.

On a battlefield in an urban area, most of the glass will already be broken so our military sniper will rarely need to consider the problem associated with shooting through glass while our police sniper will frequently find his targets standing behind glass. Not only does he need a load that will penetrate the glass, then go on to hit the target despite being deflected by the glass or going to pieces on it, but he also will need to consider the impact of flying glass on hostages or other non-criminals who may be present. A military sniper has no such concerns – in fact, the idea of being able to disable more than one enemy soldier with one shot will seem quite heart-warming.

On the flip side of course, the police sniper rarely has to worry about enemy snipers or machineguns shooting back at him or attempting to seek him out and he certainly need not worry about mortar or artillery barrages being sent over to him.

In the military, the sniper must be concerned about enemy countersniper fire whether accomplished by standard infantry troops, other snipers, artillery, or even aircraft. He typically will need to be very concerned about the exit from an area after his shot, unlike his police counterpart who typically concludes his mission with his shot. The military sniper must be prepared for many days in the field at a time unlike the police sniper who may need only to worry about a small amount of overtime after shift time. The military sniper typically will attempt to engage his targets at greater range as it is safer for shooting at a group of enemy soldiers. At 68 yards for example, a shot will immediately result in a load of enemy fire coming your way quickly. At longer ranges, the ability to find the sniper is less and hence potential danger much lower. Possibly the best thing is that the military sniper need not concern himself with pin-point accuracy at a given moment nor does he require instantaneous stopping power. He can take his shots when he finds it best to do so, and if he hits the enemy in the chest anywhere he is satisfied for he knows that the enemy soldier will be out of action for a long time even if not killed instantly. If it takes a couple of minutes to have the soldier die, it is of no consequence to the military sniper. The shooting skills of the military sniper are typically more critical, not from a pure shooting standpoint, for hitting a two-inch target at 68 yards or a 20-inch one at 680 yards requires the same inherent accuracy, but as you go out in range, you must learn how to calculate distances properly so you can adjust trajectory properly for your cartridge. It is possibly even more critical today, for since the advent of laser range finders and/or mildot scopes the military sniper must know how to judge wind. Wind that will mean nothing at 68 yards for the police sniper means a lot for the military sniper for it will be enough to completely blow the bullet off target. The ability to "read the wind" thus is an essential skill for the military sniper and it is not one that technology can help with much. Only long-term practice will develop the skill and only constant use will keep it sharp.

Equipment-wise, the military and police sniper will also differ for as the tasks are varied so also are the equipment needs.

No police sniper needs a scope with over four-power magnification and a three-power is really quite adequate. It needs to have good light-gathering abilities, but a big field of view to permit rapidly getting on to a target and following it if it moves is essential. The military sniper on the other hand needs a three-power scope occasionally but can also use a nine-power for longer shots. A good variable is useful. A good high-power is not. When pinpoint accuracy is needed today, this is more a feature of good triggers than type of action. While the bolt-action rifle typically will deliver better long-range accuracy, current semi-auto rifles are more than adequate to the tasks posed to the police sniper. A good semi-automatic rifle may very well be satisfactory. Blending in is always critical to avoid alerting the enemy to your presence, but the painted patterns on the police rifle should be different than the ones applied to the typical, rurally oriented military sniper. Bipods are typically seen on a lot of sniping rifles today but seem out of place to me. Rifles, if shot prone, would be better placed across some type of soft rest like a sand bag and if shot from other than prone, as may very well be the case, especially in the police context, such bipods alter the weapon balance, make for an awkward grip and add weight to the whole package. In the military context, the sniper is likely to shoot more prone or across improvised rests so again the bipod is not useful but the sling and its proper use are helpful to the military sniper as it will greatly improve his ability to place rounds on target.

Each rifle, whether for police or military operations, should maintain its zero. This means a stable stock, good fitting of the action to the stock, if applicable, a solid scope mounting system, and a way to carry the weapon

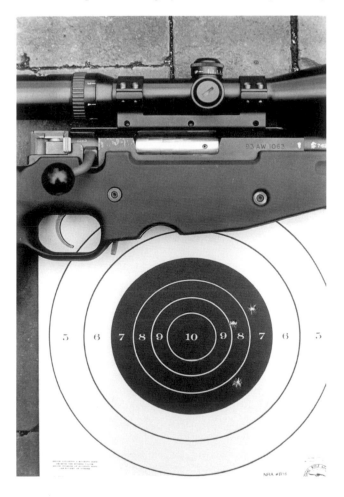

Test group shot at 505 meters by the author with Accuracy International sniper rifle with 168 gr Federal Premium ammo.

Right side view of a Soviet Dragonov sniper rifle.

practically that will keep it as safe from environmental misadventures as possible. In the police context since the weapons need to be immediately available but will only be used rarely, if ever, this means a solid metal box with foam lining to carry the weapon but some place where it will not be subject to the ravages of extreme temperature variations. Inside the vehicle is acceptable, in the trunk of a patrol car is not. For the military sniper, a large, foam-fitted metal box is simply silly. He may wish to have such a box to leave his weapon in (locked, of course) when left in the weapons room while he is on R & R (Rest and Relaxation leave) in whatever local watering spot is appropriate at the moment but in the field he will want to have his weapon immediately available and also carry as little weight as possible. Occasionally I suppose carrying the weapon in some type of fabric bag over your back while you carry a standard infantry model rifle in your hands might be sensible but my experience in the infantry field tells me that lighter is always better and carrying two rifles is simply too much to expect of our military sniper.

This point raises two interesting issues also for the military sniper. Frequently, in the field, soldiers who are carrying non-standard weapons are immediately targeted for destruction as they must be important. Just like you do not expose your binoculars or badges of rank so also carrying and being seen with a non-standard weapon is not a good idea. It will alert everyone in the area that a sniper is about and, especially in campaigns like Vietnam, this can prove quite dangerous to your military sniper. If the sniper is equipped with a bolt-action rifle, obviously his ability to defend himself in the event of enemy action being focused on him is much less than would be the case of a standard infantryman. During the Vietnam War, US Army snipers used modified M14 rifles with considerable success which still permitted them to oppose enemy attacks as well as not being seen armed with a non-standard weapon except in the eyes of the particularly well-trained observer. While such rifles give up a bit of accuracy at extreme ranges beyond say 800 yards, it was thought they made up for it at closer ranges by the benefits noted. Today with the advent of 1,000 yard-capable match rifles built on the M16 rifle and the ammunition to shoot then it would seem that no reason exists why a similar rifle could not be made for the military sniper. It would also reduce the problem of introduction of a non-standard rifle in the US armory at least and avoid the maintenance nightmare that these more accurate M14 sniper rifles created according to some sources. Reports of snipers in Vietnam equipped with M16A1 rifles topped by 3–9x variable power scopes doing excellent work out to 600 yards have been made. With today's flat-top M16 rifles, better bullets, and barrels, it should be no trouble to get equal or better performance out to 1,000 yards. Beyond that, I believe a more powerful rifle should be used but the numbers of such shots which are likely to be missed are so minimal as to be unimportant.

The author with a Remington M40A1 sniper rifle.

British military sniper testing the new Accuracy International sniper rifle now replacing the L42A1 in the British military services.

Military snipers, unlike their police counterparts, may be used to disable enemy high-value property targets in addition to personnel. This is where the current rash of 50 caliber sniping rifles becomes very handy. The cartridge is big enough to deliver a lot of power on distant targets. The projectiles can carry a good load of incendiary or explosive material to add property destruction. For targets such as radar installations, aircraft and missiles, engaging them at 2,500 or more yards may be clearly feasible. A few rounds fired into a military installation of such distances can do a lot of damage and the effect of them is to require a much greater security area around a military installation than was common in the past. This of course is good also as it ties up a lot of troops who otherwise would be fighting to provide the security, rather as the early World War II Commando attacks in France caused Hitler to tie up a lot of troops providing security against these attacks which, of course for the most part, never came. A perfect example of the sniper in a military Special Operations. A specialized weapon used by a specially trained soldier giving much greater impact to the effort than typically would be obtained by one or two soldiers. As an aside, the 50 caliber sniping rifle (or 12.7 or even 14.5 mm) can be effectively left behind without concern when exiting the area to flee retribution as the weapons are themselves of little value without proper training in their use and special matchgrade ammunition. If really concerned, pull the bolt and leave with it in the backpack. I wish the enemies you are likely to be encountering good luck in trying to make a bolt for your McMillian 50 rifle!

Chapter 8: Sniping in Special Operations – police v military

Snipers are very important elements in Special Operations. Their skill and equipment will permit them to accomplish tasks that either would require a lot more individuals or would perhaps be impossible without them. Certainly their presence may avoid unnecessary casualties and damages. While at first glance the skills and equipment of the police and military sniper may seem the same, they are actually quite different. While many military snipers will leave the service and naturally gravitate to police work and then get assigned as the police sniper, the tasks to be performed are as different as those of the infantryman and the patrol officer. While some crossover exists, they are different and require different skills, equipment, and tactics. Most critically they require the parties to recognize the differences and not confuse the two dissimilar tasks.

Chapter 9

Non-firearm Special Operations weapons

While most people view firearms as the standard Special Operations weapons (and indeed they are), there are also many situations which require non-typical weapons or when such things can be effectively utilized.

Naturally most of these situations involve military Special Operations weapons where the threshold for the use and extent of violence is much lower than in civilian Special Operations situations but that is not always the case.

Possibly the easiest to discuss are the edged weapons. Among civilian teams, a sharp knife is always handy to cut the various things that will pop up from time to time such as dangling ropes and seat belts. It is hard for me to

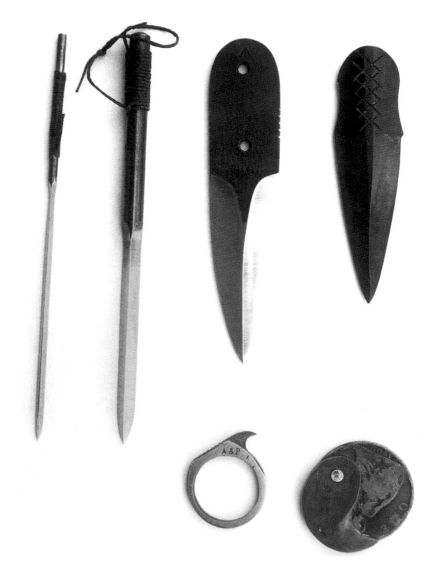

A variety of edged weapons in use by World War II special operators.

The Applegate/Fairbairn folder is quite handy for a wide variety of cutting jobs.

see any legitimate situation where a civilian Special Operator might use an attack knife. This is in counterposition to the civilian police undercover agent who may be armed with a knife when it would not be feasible to use a handgun. Criminal Investigative Command Agents familiar to the author who worked in Holland out of Western Germany in the early 1970s investigating Chinese importation of heroin often carried a knife as they were prohibited from carrying handguns in Holland. Rather than being unarmed, they would carry a knife. One CW3 investigator of the author's acquaintance got stabbed repeatedly and learned his lesson which was picked up on by others. Similarly in some undercover situations, a knife might be a better weapon to blend in with your "cover" than a firearm. But while occasionally Special Operators will work in such capacities for the most part, what is needed is a sharp, easily available knife, not a long, pointed-edged weapon suitable for "slitting throats." The key thing in such situations is to have the knife instantly available. Taping it in your assault harness is a good approach as is using a clip or knife in your pocket that is an automatic opener (switchblade) so it can be opened rapidly with only one hand.

The military operator on the other hand will typically want to have a more combat-designed knife available, backed up by some type of folding "boy-scout" type knife that can be used for all of those mundane tasks which occur in the field. Any time a combat knife is to be carried, the person who is using it should be taught the proper skills to maximize the effectiveness of the weapon. Occasionally in such situations as noted above, you will see large Bowie-style knives or stilletto-style blades. Neither is really suitable. The famed Fairbairn-Sykes fighting knife that is almost a symbol of the Special Operator of the World War II era allied was really quite fragile. The tip all too often broke off when subject to severe stabbing. The large-size Bowie knife is an excellent fighting tool but the long blade makes it somewhat unwieldy and more critically heavy. I think a proper fighting knife should be longer than a hunting knife (which never needs to be over three inches) yet shorter than a

Special Operations: weapons & tactics

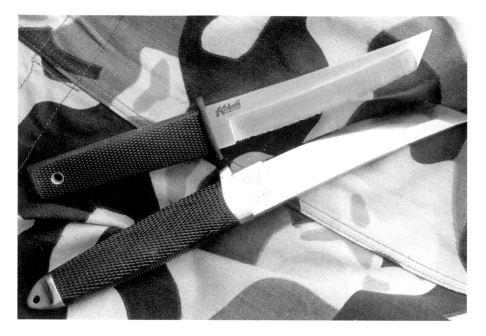

full-size Bowie. I think the K-Bar length or even the shorter pilot survival knife is more than sufficient. Quality of metal, so it will take and hold an edge you can administer in the field and not break when you strike bone, is critical.

Other specialty knives seen in Special Operations unit may reflect the native heritage of many unit members like the Kukri and Machete. Others may wish to look at the Applegate-designed "Smatchet" which, of course, is a modification of the World War I Welch short sword. The Smatchet is a typical heavy cutting tool like the Kukri but it also can be used for stabbing. The ever-present bayonet is also not bad if of an origin in the last 30 years or so when the World War I mandated length of 15 or more inches has been reduced to fighting knife length.

Other Special Operations edged weapons are also commonly found in front line infantry units. Such things as a helmet and sharpened shovel are helpful. The military operator will also carry a good supply of Claymore mines to put out toward the enemy when resting to preclude anyone coming up to his position.

Missing from line operations but found occasionally in military Special Operations units that penetrate deep behind the lines are items like bows and arrows, crossbows and air guns/blow guns. This typically comes up in places of the world where the Special Operator deals with primitive locals who are working with them but I suppose occasionally arises elsewhere. During World War II, there was a well-known English Commando Officer who supposedly killed one or more Germans with his longbow and no doubt the crossbow could be used equally well. One could suppose the blow gun would also be effective given proper poisons in certain types of attacks where guards needed to be immobilized.

More typical, however, are a variety of blunt instruments. Both civilian and military operations personnel can effectively use them. Among civilian operators, the ASP baton is well known as, of course, are simple fighting sticks as well as the more effective side-handle batons. All of these items are

A variety of "combat sheath knives." The lower one is the "Attack-Survival" by Randall, acceptable for SP use, but the top two are too heavy for my tastes.

seen occasionally in military units but also there are found more deadly coshes with spring type arms that contain a solid metal ball at the top. When utilized by the Special Operator, the metal ball is propelled with sufficient velocity to penetrate a human skull. Excessive for civilian operators but dandy in the military. The first of these was apparently taken from London subway coaches where they hung from the ceilings to permit a handhold while standing. I instantly recognized them on my first visit to the London tube. I know other types of military-type coshes include clubs that also contain knife blades that can be propelled out at speed under spring or gas pressure, socks filled with sand (or soap bars) have also been used in emergencies.

Plastic or ceramic knives (or similar non-magnetic metal knives) are also

The lower knife is the Fairbairn Sykes of World War II fame; the upper ones are Applegate Fairbairns, which developed and improved the original design.

Special Operations: weapons & tactics

The famed kukri, more of a tool than a weapon.

handy weapons for Special Operators who are assigned tasks that may put them in areas of the world where they are likely to encounter metal detectors. Again, this seems more likely to involve military teams than civilian operators, although I suppose you could conjure up a situation where a civilian Special Operator could utilize them but it seems quite distant. Naturally these types of things come in handy also when probing for land mines and other things that will detonate if you use a magnetic probe.

Naturally, as with any type of weapon, if you are going to authorize or issue it, you must provide proper training with it both to make the operator safe in his handling it as well as to maximize the benefits to be obtained from using the weapon. There are specialty instructors teaching the use of edged weapons and clubs/stick fighting just like there are for firearms. A person in charge of training would be wise to seek out such experts and utilize the unique skills and years of experience such individuals can bring to the subject. But as with firearms, it is not the titles that may have been won with them but hard learned combat skills that are sought. To teach such skills, man-on-man contact is best as it is both realistic and breeds aggression which is critically important when such direct contact weapons are used. The various "Red Man" outfits commonly seen in US law enforcement training centers of the more enlightened outlook are excellent training tools as you can then get the direct no-holds-barred contact you need. Naturally, training versions of clubs, knives and similar tools are available to help minimize the injuries that are otherwise likely to occur. But as with all training, a level of injury might well be expected when you are training high-speed Special Operators and as long as the injuries are not gratuitous but needed to get the realistic training that will save lives, it is acceptable.

Close-combat shooting techniques

Chapter 10

When discussing close combat-shooting techniques, we are dealing with distances from right off the muzzle to perhaps 100 yards. Of course, the type of weapon used may affect the distances involved. For instance, a 100-yard shot with a rifle may be viewed as close combat shooting, while one with a handgun obviously is not. The key to the whole issue is to be able to hit a target bigger than a fist and smaller than a head from the muzzle forward to 100 yards within one second. To do this requires mastering close-combat shooting techniques.

Possibly the best manual for this type of work is in the Vietnam War-era manual entitled *Training Text 12-71-1 Principles of Quick Kill* (May 1967). The books by Ed McGivern *Fast and Fancy Revolver Shooting*, Ernie Lind *The Complete Books of Trick and Fancy Shooting* and Mike Jennings *Instinct Shooting* also are excellent guides. The "Quick Kill" technique was taught to individual US Army soldiers to show them how to quickly get on their targets with their rifles and hit the enemy. In the jungles of Vietnam, these skills were incredibly important and obviously needed, but these same skills are actually

The author on the right instructs one of his officers in 1976 on instinctive shooting skills during a range program he devised.

Special Operations: weapons & tactics

One of the author's CID agents responding to an attack during a range program run in 1976; the exercise emphasizes close-range shooting.

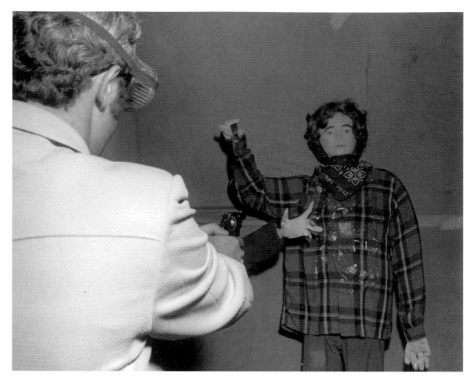

The author firing from a Glock G18 machine pistol – note the aggressive stance necessary for the effective use of such a weapon.

needed anywhere combat occurs. Enemy soldiers (and criminals) tend to appear in unanticipated areas for very short periods of time and are generally moving. They certainly will not appear as bull's eye targets do on the range nor even as man targets on field firing ranges.

When I was at Fort Benning, Georgia, in 1968, I well remember taking a Quick Kill course. Most people quickly got to the stage they could hit BB's thrown in the air with BB guns or later M14 rifles. These same skills can be mastered with the handgun also resulting in a very fast response time when confronted with enemy targets.

The proper technique is not based on foot work, for any method that requires the shooter to assume a standard position and will always ultimately fail when the shooter is caught in a different position. Nor is it dependent on hand position for the same reason. Of course, some foot and hand positions are better than others for recoil absorption and repeat shots but close-quarter combat shooting is not based on fancy foot or hand work.

The key elements are familiarity with your weapon and watching a point on your target. If you are familiar with how your weapon feels in your hands, on your cheek and shoulder (in the case of a shoulder-fired weapon) and then train yourself to look at a point on the target, not just at the target generally but a specific point like a button, you will soon find you will hit that button or be very close to it. The beauty of this system is that you can make these shots fast against indistinct moving targets.

To help you rapidly recover from the impact of recoil for follow-up shots or other targets, the shooter must be aggressive in his weapon stances. He must

The author firing an M1921 Thompson SMG, viewed from both right and left sides. Note the aggressive stance, the high elbow and foot placement add recoil control and accuracy on the target. A similar stance is used for proper combat firing with auto-loader or revolver.

Special Operations: weapons & tactics

An aggressive stance is useful to master the combat shotgun.

The author test-firing the Ithica featherweight 20 gauge 13½" barrel.

Forward aggressive stance as used with the DA revolver.

Author firing Heckler & Koch MP5 equipped with streamlight flashlight forearm. Note 3 empties in the air and the flash flying upwards from the Vector round that impacted the plate.

Author firing 357 Magnum M66 Smith & Wesson while running sideways against the target. Note both feet are in the air and the smoke coming from the weapon. Instinctive firing skills will permit the shooter to get good results at these ranges.

lean forward into the weapon much as if he were stabbing the target with a knife or bayonet on the end of the weapon. Doing so will help offset the recoil felt and allow much more rapid repeat shots. Typically I find that I see my sights in the lower field of my vision as mere dark objects that help me line up my weapon more readily. James Cirillo of the old famed New York Stake-Out Squad calls this method the Cirillo Point but many people (including myself) used it for years before Jim put his name on it. In fact, I think mastering it is one reason why the old, thin, dark and narrow sights seen on so many handguns until the last 20 years made no difference in their combat performance. A properly trained shooter did not use them anyway so the fact that they were poor sights made no difference. When shooting a shoulder-fired weapon, the shooter also watches a point on the target looking over his sights. Shotgunners do this all the time with their shotguns and riflemen/ submachinegunners can do the same thing on their human targets with equally good results. With practice I find that I am able to hit flying clay pigeons which are both smaller and much faster than any human target with an SMG possibly 30% of the time and get very close the rest of the time. If I shoot six-inch "rolling rabbit" type targets, my percentages go up substantially as they are not side on toward you but rather the flat (large) side to you. A few hundred shots fired at such things with handguns, rifles or SMGs will soon make any shooter a faster, deadlier shot.

After explaining the technique, the next step is to go out and practice it. Unfortunately, many range programs are dominated by people who are

Chapter 10: Close-combat shooting techniques

experts at formal target shooting and the idea of not using the sights and hitting moving targets is foreign to them. Such people need to be educated to the reality of close-combat shooting or replaced with those who understand it.

Some realistic goals for our shooting program of hitting something bigger than your fist but smaller than your head in one second may well be up to 50 feet for handguns, 50 yards for SMGs, and 100 yards for rifles. Faster is always better than smaller as long as you are still on the head-size target; if you are hitting smaller than the fist you are taking too long, obviously. Twenty-two rimfire weapons are good, cheap training weapons for this type of practice which can be ammo intensive; Hornady Vector ammo, which has an element in the butt of the bullet which glows like a light beam, is similarly handy. There are also one-place laser sights on your weapon which may very well prove really useful, and not just gimmick.

Chapter 11

Night-vision/laser-sighting devices and other sighting aids

Typically, weapons used by Special Operations groups utilize iron sights or telescopic sights. In past days, the telescopic sights were used on sniping rifles almost exclusively, but with the recent advance of highly durable, non-iron sights like the Elcan and ACOG, not to mention the AUG sight by Steyr, these types of sights are beginning to appear on typical battle rifles and even SMGs. Also, reflex-type sights, which project a red dot only, are encountered and small reflex types that can be mounted on a pistol are beginning to be seen. It is possible in the years ahead that they will become common on real carry handguns as they get smaller. They are actually seen nowadays on rifles/SMGs used in combat. Such reflex sights – if you can use them (not everyone can) – are quite quick as they allow you to shoot easily with both eyes open and permit you to focus on the target as you should when shooting at real assailants, and not on the sights.

At the same time as these sights have been developed, we have also seen the radical advance in the area of radioactive "glow in the dark" night sights. About 25 years ago, when these first came out, they were rare and difficult to install. Today they are almost commonplace. I have some real doubts about their value on police handguns, since shooting in conditions of near total darkness is not a practice to be encouraged, and the shooter will typically be

Left-side view of AUG 9 x 19 mm.

Above: The author firing the AUG 9 x 19 mm SMG

Left: The author with Heckler & Koch Fabarm Tactical 1299 equipped with PW Point optical sight.

Special Operations: weapons & tactics

Kydex holster with Heckler & Koch USP with flashlight unit.

watching his target not his sights anyway. There the money spent on radioactive sights is likely better spent on spare ammo for training and mini flashlights to be carried by the officer to assist him illuminating the target. Even better in that regard is the idea of a permanently mounted flashlight on the weapon to be used to illuminate the subject. They are now of a size that such a weapon/flashlight combo can be carried as a duty weapon rather than a specialty raid weapon or carried in an awkward, belt-mounted pouch. Radioactive night sights are better on shoulder-mounted weapons that will be used at a distance; military Special Operators, who may very well be called to shoot in total darkness and will be unconcerned by the issue of innocents being hit (since by definition for them, being behind enemy lines and facing a military foe, everyone is a legitimate target) will find them very useful. The one drawback I see, except for costs (and one less jet fighter will pay for all the radioactive night sights in all Special Operations units worldwide in all

A British soldier during the Falklands War with a second generation night-vision scope mounted on his L1A1. He is escorting Argentine prisoners.

likelihood) is that you can see them in the dark from the back. This was totally brought home to me when I was in a Ranger platoon going forward and noticed a green glow on the back of everyone's hat where the "cat eyes" were. A good way to keep track of your platoon members but possibly a little too good for your enemy who may very well be behind you at some time on a confusing battlefield.

Besides the types of sights I have mentioned, other types of useful sights in Special Operations units are night-vision type sights and laser units. A night-vision unit, of course, merely magnifies existing light so that the shooter can then use his conventional sights to align his weapon. In Vietnam, early examples of such "starlight scopes" were seen and represented a major breakthrough. They were big, heavy, and cost a lot of money. Today, the best teams are well into fourth generation units and they have become better and cheaper. Any Special Operations unit that anticipates operating in low light situations should have access to such technology. They can allow you to place your rounds on target in what appears to be near total darkness. Typically they are mounted on rifles and LMGs although goggles worn by the operator will permit the operator to utilize standard handguns and maybe even an SMG if fired from the shoulder point position. All such goggles I have seen or used are heavy and awkward, so the utility of them seems quite open to question in my mind although the future may be better. The normal type of weapon sights of the best current generation, on the other hand, are quite useful and no team, be it military or civil, should be without it.

While not seen too frequently any more, occasionally infra-red sighting units are seen. These send out a path of infra-red light which is, of course,

Special Operations: weapons & tactics

Flashlight attachment as developed during World War II for use by British or Imperial forces – an interesting development showing that the idea of flashlights on an SMG is not a modern SWAT innovation. The diagram shows the additional fittings required, a spotlight projector bracket, a clip trigger guard and a lead clip.

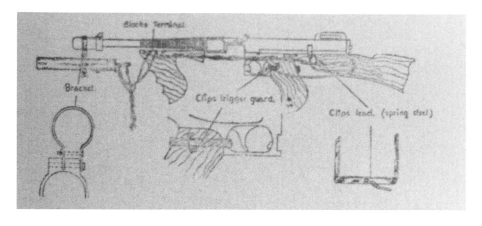

Right-side view of the 40 UMP Heckler & Koch SMG with stock folded.

beyond the normal spectrum of human eyes and you have a mechanism you use that will allow you to transform such light beams into a visible presence. Unfortunately you can easily see people who use such devices with a night-vision scope or if you have an infra-red scope yourself. As a consequence, they are not seen too much anymore, although for clearing areas where white light would not be useful as it would disclose your presence readily and no natural light is present (a cave or tunnel is a good example), such things might prove

MP5 9 x 19mm (top) and UMP .40 (below), both fitted with white light sources.

useful. After a team has bought every other near useful tool, an infra-red scope might be handy.

More commonly encountered today are laser sights. These are like radioactive sights in some regards. About 25 years ago, I knew a man who developed laser sights for handguns. They were as big as a multiple cell flashlight and as heavy. They also were very expensive and did not seem to hold their zero on weapons well or hold up. It was kind of neat to see a laser beam projected on a distant target however. Over the next 25 years, laser sighting devices have gotten much smaller and cheaper. Now they are sufficiently small to fit into the guide rod of a Glock pistol or be fitted to the side of a pair of grips. The batteries to operate them are small enough to be typically used in hearing aid devices. They can be had in a variety of colors so different members of the Special Operation team can each have his own color and thereby tell who is pointing his weapon at what target and, of course, it is still fun to see the laser dot projected on to some distant target.

Unfortunately, lasers do not do what they seem to do in the advertisements. They fail to project a visible beam through the air unless the air is filled with some smoking substances sufficient to cause the light beam of the laser to be reflected on the material. It would be nice if a solid red or similar color beam went from your weapon like a light saber in "Star Wars" to your target but

Ruger P94 DAO police model with integral laser under the barrel, left-hand (top) and right-hand view (below).

alas that is not the case. Instead what the laser does is project a small dot on the subject. Unfortunately the dots are small and hard to pick up in normal light, though better in the dark. In daylight, they are almost invisible beyond 15 yards in my experience, in fact. At night, they can be picked up at 200

Chapter 11: Night-vision/laser-sighting devices and other sighting aids

Left-side view of a Heckler & Koch USP equipped with a tactical light – a nice bedside or raid gun.

Glock 34 with factory 33-round magazine with M3 light installed.

yards, I have found, but it is slow picking them up. If you have multiple shooters present, then obviously you need to have different colors for each shooter as otherwise I may confuse your laser with mine and, thinking the pistol is on target, fire it resulting in a wild shot endangering innocents and friends alike. Occasionally people write of the intimidation value of a laser but that seems very unlikely to me. I cannot see it unless I look down on my chest to see it. What I can see is the red (or other color) laser diode beaming in my direction. I can then use it as an aiming point for my fire at you. Not a very satisfactory result, in my opinion. In addition to these tactical problems, lasers use batteries which, of course, are prone to go down at the worst possible moment and this, if you have grown used to using your laser instead of your sights, may create a problem. Lasers also cost money that is better spent on training ammunition in my opinion and make the weapon either more bulky or slower to use. At a minimum , you have another switch to flip on and off which cannot certainly increase your speed of presentation.

A much better solution to this problem of shooting in darkened conditions is to use a white-light source, or in simple terms, a flashlight. The idea of using a flashlight attached to a weapon is not a new idea for Special Operations personnel by any means. During the early stages of World War II when British Commandos were staging raids all along the occupied coasts, the issue SMG, the Thompson M1921/8, was equipped with a flashlight that the shooter could flip on and off rapidly. In the environment that the British operated in of close-in raids with their SMG , this ability to quickly light up a subject and engage them with the Thompson must have been quite useful.

Today white-light sources are common on SMG and combat shotguns. Mounts to fit them to the M4 Carbine are also common, and of course any rifle or other weapon that uses that rail system common today can quickly be fitted with a white-light system. While a white-light source does cost money to buy and maintain and can be broken, it is such a useful feature when added to the Special Operator's weapon that it is hard to see how any unit can justify not having such devices. The military team possibly may have less use for such devices simply because they tend to engage targets at greater distances than their civilian counterparts, but certainly every shoulder-fired weapon used by civilian Special Operators should have a white light attached. As some white-light sources today can be conveniently attached to a handgun, I would say all members of the civilian Special Operations team should have them affixed to their handguns also. Civilian Special Operators generally operate at closer ranges and the ability to quickly evaluate a presented threat and engage it if necessary are if anything more critical in the civilian context. I think all weapons carried in the primary handgun role should be white-light-equipped at all times in addition to having them installed on all shoulder weapons – except sniper rifles. While it is not true that you cannot hit what you cannot see, it is true that you are more likely to hit the correct thing and hit it hard if you can see it. The white-light source mounted on the Special Operator's weapon makes the accomplishment of this task much less difficult.

Specialized ammunition

Chapter 12

Firearms of whatever type and description are merely missile launchers. It is not so important what weapon is used frequently as what projectile it launches in the accomplishment of many missions. To keep matters as simple as possible, let us call specialized ammunition anything using other than conventional full-metal-jacket, lead-filled projectiles in any cartridge.

On this definition, perhaps the first type to be discussed is the standard hollow point or expanding top round. These projectiles are designed to expand on impact with the target and thereby release their energy in a more rapid fashion. This hopefully will incapacitate the target more rapidly and additionally minimize the risk to others, since they will not exit from the person who was the intended target and thus endanger others behind or to the side of them.

Such projectiles can be made out of lead in combination with tin to get different rates of expansion or can be a jacketed bullet filled with lead. Such projectiles are banned from use in warfare between nations but are not prohibited by The Hague Convention of 1908 when used in a law-enforcement context of counterterrorist operations. To use them in a military operation, however, does violate the International Law of War and would subject the user (as well as those authorizing their use) to criminal prosecution.

While many at this point will roll their eyes and make odd noises about this type of restriction, keep in mind that it is the law and you violate it at your own risk. Fortunately, this very effective anti-personnel ammunition can be used in many anti-terrorist operations that are foisted off on military groups. Additionally, in military operations, the low penetration of such ammunition becomes a drawback, as in true military operations what is frequently wanted is *more* penetration, and concern about damage to innocents is quite marginal, since by the time conventional troops are in battle positions, those who can leave the area generally have done so. Hence restrictions on the military use of such ammunition are not usually a problem.

Another type of specialized projectile that is useful in Special Operations is the armor-piercing round. This typically has a copper jacket surrounding a steel penetrator of some type. Such rounds will prove substantially better at penetrating hard targets than conventional ball rounds. They become quite useful for shooting vehicles of the soft-skin types such as trucks as well as those who ride in or hide behind. Good AP Rifle ammunition will also have a real effect on helicopters and aircraft that move slowly enough to be damaged by any small arms fire. AP rounds will penetrate jungle and wooden defensive positions of the enemy to a greater extent than ball rounds. Additionally you can cut through walls in buildings that your opponent may be hiding behind in urban areas, so that while you may not be able to see them, you can shoot down the wall around him and thereby hopefully hit him also. In urban areas, when doors are frequently booby-trapped or become an obvious target for your enemy, a short burst with an LMG loaded with AP rounds will allow you to cut a hole in the wall to crawl through instead of using the door. Naturally it works equally well going into a building as it does leaving one.

Special Operations: weapons & tactics

Entrance hole (top) of 5.56 x 45 mm (SS109) on a US GI helmet fired at 50 yards. The exit hole caused as it came out the other side is shown below.

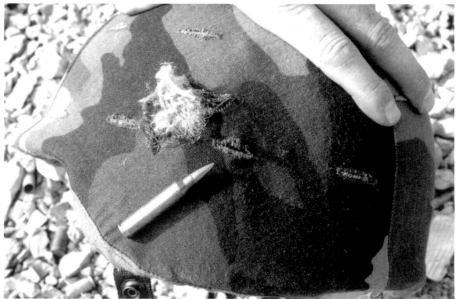

Tracer ammunition which consists of a burning element in the tail of a bullet is also quite useful for a number of reasons. It can be used to alert you to the fact you are getting to the end of a magazine or belt of ammunition so you know it is time to restock your weapon. It can be used to set items on fire that you suspect may contain enemy equipment or men or which provides cover for them you wish to deny them. You can also use it to start fires to shelter your movement into or out of the area so as to keep the enemy busy confronting the consequences of a fire as well as your actions. It may provide greater stopping power on individual targets. My colleagues who are in the position to say "yes" tell me so but fortunately I cannot say from experience at either end of the question. Naturally it can be used to guide your troops or

Right-side view of the Heckler & koch P95 "Navy SEAL" 9 x 19 with suppressor.

any incoming aircraft to a position you wish them to hit. It can also be used to coordinate attacks especially if you utilize different color tracers at different times. This can be especially useful where communications are difficult to achieve or subject to monitoring by the enemy. Tracer ammunition comes in different colors and is often designed to burn at different intervals. Some will not burn until a certain number of yards out of the barrel to avoid the enemy tracing it right back to the shooter while others burn right out the barrel. Some tracer ammunition will change colors as it burns so it will mark distances in this fashion. I have never had the call to use that type of tracer ammunition, but it could I suppose be very useful especially in areas where long-range suppression fire techniques were called for by ground-positioned LMGs.

Incendiary ammunition contains a pill of flammable material in the bullet which will go forward when the bullet strikes the targets, throwing out burning material in all directions and causing fires. This becomes very useful when wanting to destroy objects that are flammable, and can be quite dandy in vehicle ambushes as an incendiary hits the metal, lights up the tire, and the burning tire will destroy the vehicle so it is not necessary to hit the gas tank, although that is best.

Incendiary ammunition is rarely used by design against human targets, although I suppose it would be useful against enemy soldiers in body armor as it would cause their body armor to light up causing them to discard it lest they get toasted.

Naturally, ammunition combining these features is available and such ammunition as Czech armor-piercing incendiary tracers is well regarded among my friends who like to engage in vehicle ambushes. A belt in an RPD is, I am told, quite dandy for such a use.

Typically ammunition should be as speedy as possible given pressure considerations as this helps to lower the trajectory. However, bullets that exceed the speed of sound (usually calculated at 1100 fps as a convenient figure) will give a ballistic crack as they pass your enemy. From this they can locate your position and bring fire to bear on you. Accordingly, especially in

Left-side view of the "Navy SEAL" P9S Heckler & Koch 9mm pistol fitted with a suppressor. The sights are fitted especially to allow use when the suppressor is fitted to the pistol. The H&K locking system is compatible with the use of a suppressor unlike the Browning locking system.

Special Operations, suppressors are commonly utilized. A suppressor will muffle the muzzle blast but cannot affect the sonic boom created by the supersonic projectile as it passes the target. By reducing the velocity below the speed of sound the weapon can effectively be nearly noiseless with the better grade of suppressors. With a distance of 10 yards or so, a little wind and a proper combination of suppressor, weapon modification, and ammunition, you truly cannot detect some rounds as they are fired at you. Even if the quality does not reach that level, it is much more difficult to determine where the shooting is coming from when it is at a distance. This becomes very useful when a small unit is in an ambush setting can effectively wipe out their opponents before they respond in kind. Of course, if they respond, their conventional weapons and ammunition will permit the other enemy in the area to immediately zone in on the shooting area.

The biggest problem with subsonic ammunition besides keeping it truly subsonic given changing climactic conditions and operating elevations which of course can effect powder burning rates and hence velocity, is to make it work in self-loading weapons. It is necessary to have sufficient pressure to keep the mechanism working properly. This is done usually by using a heavier projectile. Naturally they hit to different points than conventional rounds so re-sighting is necessary. Often the pressure curve is different than exists with conventional rounds and while having the ultimate pressure necessary to function, the action will not allow the weapon to work properly. Thus careful ammunition selection is critical where suppressors are used. Naturally for limited-time Special Operations, such as police operations, which typically are of very short duration, this is not a major problem. In military units, where the duration of action may be much longer, keeping an adequate supply in the channels can prove to be quite challenging. Without their specialized ammunition, the suppressors are much less useful, unfortunately.

Most times the ability to either deeply penetrate a target medium or expand to an increasingly large size is an important characteristic of ammunition but especially in some types of Special Operations, it is desirable to have ammunition that will quickly render a target *hors de combat* but not penetrate sensitive material. An example might be work in or around airplanes, nuclear power plants, objects of great value and similar things. For these uses, the frangible round has been developed. It is generally made out of a copper jacket filled with either powdered copper material held together with some type of binder or very small size shot. The Glaser and Mag-Safe rounds are common examples of the latter breed and the GreenShield is the most common example of the former. Both rounds will give either excellent, or at least acceptable, stopping power on human targets yet have minimum penetration on hard targets. As with other specialty rounds, getting them to function in self-loading weapons is always a problem. They frequently are lighter than standard projectiles, and getting the necessary pressure to properly function a self-loading action can be very difficult at times. However, it can be done. Similarly sometimes the nose shape is such that feeding in some weapons, especially military-style weapons set up for conventional ball ammunition shaped projectiles, can be a challenge. Again it can be done but you must take care to check each weapon with the ammunition as often seemingly identical weapons will differ in their ability to utilize the ammunition.

Despite these drawbacks, if done properly, frangible ammunition will allow the Special Operator to accomplish tasks safely that otherwise might pose such a high danger risk in the event of a mishap that no action could be undertaken.

While we have discussed various specialty ammunition which have a lot of dissimilar features, one common feature of many specialty rounds is that their accuracy level may fall below the standard that is needed. For especially good accuracy, true match-quality ammunition is needed. This is ammunition that frequently has the same style of projectile as a conventional military round or it may use the type of top commonly called expanding point or hollow point. Whatever style of projectile is used, however, the key to this type of specialty cartridge is that it will permit a higher degree of accuracy to be obtained in a weapon than a conventional round. It accomplishes this by reducing the variables of case size, capability, powder load, bullet weight and balance to a minimum. By reducing these variables, those things that tend to cause inaccuracy are minimized and the results will be better. This can often improve accuracy considerably. For instance, in a very accurate .308 rifle, the groups at 100 yards with match ammunition may well be less than one-half inch, while standard ball rounds run two inches and some specialty rounds perhaps six inches. All from the same rifle and shooter. If top-notch accuracy is needed due to distant target or small-size match ammo is called for whether in rifle or handgun.

So far the ammunition we have been discussing is designed to be used in rifled weapons. Shotguns, however, are a fertile area for specialized ammunition. Naturally there are the standard buckshot and slug loads so familiar to everyone. But others are also commonly encountered. Cartridges loaded with rubber pellets for crowd control are helpful when trying to leave an area after a raid when you do not wish to injure the local population but do not want them to overwhelm you either. Similarly rounds that go down range then explode with a loud "bang" may help clear unruly areas. Shells loaded to act as flash-bang devices help the Special Operator enter a room when it may not be feasible to throw in a distraction device. Projectiles filled with dye or similar coloring to mark unruly parties for later pick-up by the authorities are encountered also. Among the most useful of specialized ammunition types are the rounds designed to blow locks from doors yet go to pieces on the other side of the door to avoid endangering the room occupants. Many Special Operations teams carried a short-barreled repeating shotgun typically with a muzzle stand-off device to blow locks (or hinges) off doors to allow a rapid entry. A most excellent technique.

Varieties of less useful shotgun specialty ammunition occasionally seen also include flechettes (too light and few in number to be effective), bolo style buckshot (an idea that has never worked too well), mixed small- and large-size shot (co-called Malaysian loads due to their original use out there during the emergency in the 1950s) which seem of little use to me unless you are interested in inflicting light wounds on the enemy that will get infected in the jungle environment, and, of course, tear-gas shells which have so little capacity that they are unlikely to be of any real usefulness, although shot into a vehicle they sometimes may prove helpful.

Weapons are merely projectile launchers and it makes no difference whether they are in the hands of a traditional soldier or a police officer or a Special Operator, they are still merely launchers. Standard ammunition is capable of doing most common tasks required from projectile weapons but there are occasions when a specialty round will come in very handy at performing a job that could otherwise not be done or done only with great difficulty with conventional ammunition. When that time comes, like the Special Operator himself, it is time to bring out the special ammunition.

Chapter 13

Ballistic armor – wearing it and defeating it

In the last 25 years or so, a virtual revolution has taken place in ballistic armor, whether the type to be worn over the body or on the head. Richard Davis of The Second Chance Safety Vest Company really must be given the most credit for these developments. Davis took the armored vest concept as it came out of the Korean War – as a bulky, heavy, external vest designed to stop artillery fragments – and converted it into a concealable, relatively comfortable vest capable of stopping the typical handgun ammunition fired at US police officers. In doing so, he, without a doubt, saved hundreds of lives on both sides of the law, for not only were the police officers saved but also the criminal was only an attempted murderer, not a "cop killer", so the result typically was a short prison sentence after which possibly he was rehabilitated rather than having a capital murder conviction resulting in a minimum of life imprisonment or death.

Once Davis showed it could be made, an attempt was made to improve the vests used by military units also. There, of course, a different problem existed, as the typical military encounter involves full-jacketed, possibly steel-core, rifle-power-level rounds, and, unlike police operations, military operations take place under extremely hostile environmental conditions and are of long term duration. This substantially limits their use in conventional military units. Special Operations, whether military or civilian in nature, typically are of shorter duration so the use of such heavy rifle-proof armor is not totally out of line. As such missions frequently are inserted by air and leave by helicopter, the weight penalty is not as high a hurdle for our Special Operators. Unfortunately even with the best-technology, rifle-proof armor is heavy (around 30 pounds), awkward and hot. But for short duration missions, it may very well be acceptable, although I must say I am dubious, except for police operations. Military operations of even short duration can be several hot, weary days while police operations are frequently measured in hours if not minutes for actual periods of contact when the vest must be worn. Similarly the extra gear that a police Special Operator must carry is much less than that found with the military Special Operator, and the weight penalty is not critical for the police special officer.

Light-weight, concealable armor falls very much in the same category – useful for police but of limited use in military Special Operations. Police Special Operations may very well encounter the upset husband or felony arrest raid where typical handgun weapons or shotguns are to be encountered. Fortunately, less than five per cent of police shootings take place using rifle-powered weapons although attempts to restrict handgun sales always has the effect of increasing the use of rifles, I believe, for attacks on officers. Attempts to restrict handgun sales not only violate essential elemental human rights but also actually endanger police officers ultimately. The police Special Operator thus may find himself shot with a handgun. The military Special Operator, on the other hand, is likely to be shot by a rifle-powered weapon and would be indeed fortunate to be shot only with a handgun. This is especially so today as the common AKM rifle has virtually replaced the pistol-powered SMG or handgun in the hands of enemy soldiers. Even light-weight, concealable body armor is hot, heavy and awkward in the field, and my judgment would be to not wear it on military Special Operations as it is unlikely to stop anything the Special Operator is shot with in the field. I think I would rather carry more water or ammo. Or even better, just carry less weight so I could move faster and with greater energy. Of course, such vests do provide some degree of protection against artillery fragments and also grenade fragments but if a Special Operator gets into a position where artillery is brought to bear on them, they have real problems to begin with – I would take the weight savings and risk the grenade fragments. My choice, possibly not yours.

Armored helmets are another recent development. When I was in the army, I wore the famed steel pot of World War II. We all knew it would not stop a rifle bullet with a direct hit but could save your head from a glancing blow. A .45 ACP would not penetrate it (naturally we tried) but the enemy .30 (7.62 x 25 mm) pistol/SMG would go on through it. A 9 x 18 round, of course, would not penetrate it although possibly the new AP version of the 9 x 18 (Makarov) mm would go through; I do not know, not having shot any of it yet. The helmet would stop grenade and artillery fragments which, as a straight-leg infantry type, I found somewhat comforting to the extent that whenever I thought about not wearing it, I thought about a fragment hitting my head and wore it. The whole thing weighed 2¾ pounds and beat down on the shoulders and neck after a time. I found you also had to hold it on with one hand as you ran across open areas rapidly, otherwise it would fall off but World War II stories about the consequences of wearing the chin strap snapped kept me from hooking it. The most use, of course, that most soldiers had from their "steel pots" was to use them to wash, shave and otherwise handle routine bodily functions in. Not very dramatic but quite useful. I remain unclear about what US troops use for these functions in this day of one piece Kevlar helmets.

In recent years, Kevlar-based helmets have appeared and are credited with saving a number of lives in recent US campaigns; I have worn them and must say I do not find them any better or easier to wear than our old steel pots but perhaps they are a bit easier to wear when running. Naturally these helmets will not stop rifle fire. I shot the first one I had access to and found it could be readily penetrated by all rifle-level ammunition used by today's armies. Pistol ammunition (and thus SMG ammunition) would not penetrate unless it had an AP penetrator in it; then, of course, it went through both sides typically and would kill the wearer of it, obviously. Still it gave better performance than the old steel pots in this regard. I assume it will also offer better protection against glancing rifle rounds and fragments of all types. As it has no real weight penalty over the old steel pot, I see no reason why you should not wear your Kevlar helmet anywhere you wore your steel pot.

For police-style Special Operations, the Kevlar helmet is a must, although painting it some non-military color might be useful from the public relations point of view since the helmet looks a little too much like those used by Nazi soldiers in World War II for my taste.

The military Special Operator, however, falls into a different camp. The distinctive look of a helmet even at night will alert your opponent to your presence which may not be the most desirable result. The weight of the helmet

Chapter 13: Ballistic armor – wearing it and defeating it

Entrance hole (top) on a US GI Kevlar helmet caused by a 9 x 19mm round (Czech steel core penetrator) fired from a Beretta M9 at 50 feet. The entrance hole can be seen below, and the penetrator is also in the picture. Note that the bullet penetrated the helmet but did not come out the other side.

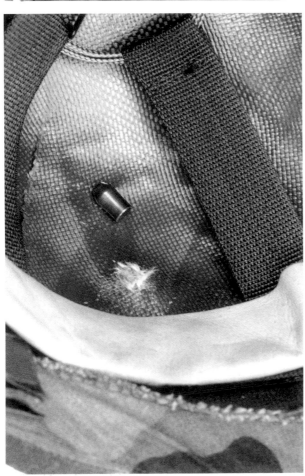

Special Operations: weapons & tactics

The author with a Heckler & Koch 53 SMG 5.56 x 45 mm. An excellent SMG and 5.56 mm short rifle design.

and the reduced hearing you get also are clear drawbacks. The protection it affords while comforting to the line infantryman who expected to be shelled by enemy artillery and mortars should not be a concern for the Special Operator. Of course, nothing in life is free and many decisions are made based on weighing factors involved and individuals will give greater or lesser weight to similar factors based on their prior experience and opinion as to future events. They then may make different conclusions about whether an item of equipment is worth taking along on a mission. I for instance would never bother to take a 9-inch Bowie knife on a patrol as I am so unlikely to use it that I prefer to avoid the weight. On the other hand, a 2-inch M60 S&W .38 revolver in the upper pocket of my fatigues I always found very comforting. So it is with the ballistic helmet for the Special Operator. My inclination would be to not take it and gain the speed and energy I would get from the less weight and awkwardness avoided.

Defeating armor, whether vests or helmets, is always a matter of increased penetration; to gain this without getting excessive recoil, you must go to greater speed with light-weight projectiles and/or use a round that will part the fabric with a sharp nose rather than trying to cut a big hole in it and also

The author with the Galil SAR with 8 x 24 plate. The only hit on the target was the first shot of a three-shot burst. The remaining rounds were totally off the plate. Fast semi-fire would be better.

not deform. If your enemy wears armor, you must be prepared to shoot through it. The idea of head shots only is simply too silly to consider. You must thus use ammunition that is capable of defeating your enemies' body armor whether in police or military operations.

In police operations, you typically will be encountering soft, concealable body armor which, while proof against typical handgun rounds used in police weapons, will not contain rifle-power loads nor AP pistol rounds. Unfortunately in police operations, the concern for over penetration is always there and great efforts to avoid shooting non-involved individuals must be made. The solution to this is to use a high-velocity round designed not to penetrate human torsos but of a small diameter so as to permit ready penetration. For our typical police entry team, a 5.56 x .45 mm weapon such as the H&K 53, Colt M4, or even shorter 11-inch variant, Steyr AUG 14-inch, Galil SAR 13½ or possibly Micro-Galil utilizing the 40 gr. JHP Federal round, is nearly ideal. It will go through concealable vests yet has less penetration in wallboard than conventional 9 x 19 mm rounds. For handguns rounds such as a French THV round will work nicely penetrating such vests yet having rapid ballistic decay and not possess too much penetration in

Right-side view of the Galil 5.56 x 45mm.

Left side view of the Heckler & Koch M93 rifle. The standard H&K M33 model is identical except for the selector lever and additional centrally mounted magazine release.

buildings. Better yet for either police or military units is the FN-designed 5.7 cartridge used in either the handgun or SMG. It has a steel penetrator in the bullet which permits penetration in concealable body armor yet tumbles when striking flesh and in my actual tests would not penetrate through a three-pound pork shoulder while still pulping the bone when struck. The FN Five-seveN pistol may be the best possible handgun for the police or even military Special Operator for these specific needs.

While the police Special Operator will be very concerned about over penetration and is unlikely to find himself facing a foe equipped with rifle-proof armor, the military Special Operator is probably going to be encountering a different problem. He is likely to be encountering conventional troops whose first- and second-level armies at least may well have effective, non-concealable rifle-proof body armor. He wants to shoot through the armor. He does not care much about over-penetration since almost by definition he is operating in enemy territory surrounded by his opponents so if he can get more than one with one shot, so much the better. On the other hand, he typically will be very concerned about having to be supplied with special ammunition which seems to have a way of not being available when needed, and he will need something that will function in his weapons. The answer for him is an AP rifle load that contains a steel penetrator. Fortunately

those are readily available in all typical rifle cartridges used today. Very few vests encountered will take a strike from an AP rifle round of the 7.62 x 51 mm power level at typical engagement distances. The only real drawback seems to be that from cartridges like the 5.56 x 45mm, when used in the AP format of SS109 and fired in a short 14½ inch barrel weapon like the M4, the bullet will not be going fast enough to tumble in a non-vested subject and small, low-performance holes will be drilled in the opponents resulting in little stopping power. Exactly this problem was encountered in the 1990's operations in Somalia apparently. The obvious answer is to substitute a 7.62 x 51mm weapon.

For handgun use, either the previously mentioned FN Five-seveN pistol by FN loaded with AP rounds is great for defeating vests or simply going to 9 mm AP projectiles. Steel-cored AP projectiles in 9 mm will go completely through US armored vests and helmets yet they comply completely with The Hague Convention of 1908. They function flawlessly in conventional weapons of all types, generate no excessive recoil, flash or blast and present only the drawback of slightly greater expense (sometimes) than ball. But, on unarmoured subjects, they will simply blast on through with stopping power being lower than what you encounter when you use expanding police-style ammunition. But then conventional military, full-metal-jacket ball is no better and can be stopped by a vest so you might as well use the AP rounds and get the benefits then with no real drawbacks.

Armor vests and helmets are issues that come up for both the police as well as the military Special Operator. The importance of the items to the Special Operator will vary depending upon the type of operation and how that individual evaluates the pros and cons of armor use. However, they determine the balance to be struck for them – they must always know how to defeat the use of those armored vests and helmets when encountered in the field worn by their opponents. It can be done with a little prior thought and planning on the subject.

Heckler & Koch 53 5.56 x 45 mm SMG. Far superior to the H&K MP5 for both power and long-range accuracy. A better weapon for urban use; also good for lower penetration with proper ammunition.

Chapter 14

The urban v. rural battlefield in Special Operations

Typically when considering the difference between urban and rural Special Operations battlefields, there is a tendency to view the urban battlefield as a short-range fighting area of short duration while the rural battlefield will find action taking place over longer ranges and periods of time. To an extent, this is, of course, true, but not always by any means. Similarly there is a general thought that civilian Special Operators work in the urban area and the military Special Operator typically handles the rural situations. Again true to an extent but not always.

With the growth of the drug trade in the rural areas in countries as diverse as the United States and Colombia, a civilian law enforcement Special Operations team is likely to be encountering rural operations. They must be prepared for such things. Similarly the arrival of well-financed terrorist groups in urban areas, who are entitled to be treated as legitimate belligerents and thus can also be legitimate targets for the military Special Operator, can find those teams working in urban areas. They likewise must be trained to handle such things. A rural law-enforcement task may take several days or weeks to conduct depending on surveillance needs while an urban military operation may well be over in a matter of seconds. Thus it is neither the locale of the battlefield nor the duration of the mission that sets such actions apart.

What mainly distinguishes these battlefields will be the legal restrictions that are placed on the teams. These considerations are more fully detailed in another chapter. Here it is sufficient to note that in broadest possible terms, the civilian operator seeks to use the minimum amount of justifiable force he can to achieve his goals: these are stopping aggressive acts, ending the criminal operation and capturing his subjects with an eye to prosecuting them in a Court of Law where they will be afforded all the protections of the criminal justice system in that particular country. All civilian operation activities, wherever they take place, will occur with these goals in mind, ever thoughtful that the operator's own actions are subject to thorough investigation by the authorities both on the criminal as well as civil level. The military Special Operator generally has a much less involved task. His goal is typically to seize an area or free an area of belligerents, capturing or killing as many of them as possible in the process as the opportunity presents itself, limited by the desire to sustain minimal casualties among members of his own unit, restrained solely by the possibility of criminal prosecution for violations of the International Law of War but totally unconcerned about potential individual civil liability. This lack of concern about civil liability, strict criminal liability, building a prosecutable case against an individual and freedom from criticism for damage inflicted on persons or property, unless way over the top, can be quite liberating to the members of a military Special Operations group.

I think it is safe to say the mission is physically harder on the military Special Operator. Their missions typically take longer, they are isolated often behind enemy lines facing a hostile population on all sides and have little available support. They often have to travel long distances over land or enter by sea and are confronted by a professional enemy who will attempt to bring everything modern science can deliver to kill them. They often know that, should they be captured, in many situations, they will be exposed to brutal treatment ending in a sudden death. Because of all these factors, the military Special Operator typically is younger and fitter than his civilian counterparts, although not always by any means. He does, of course, have a great advantage over his civilian counterpart in that his missions will typically be for defined periods. In other words, the time between missions may well be in training but the stress of day-to-day confrontation will be missing. The civilian operator typically will not need to travel long distances to his target although occasionally it may occur. He, of course, knows that help is available should things go really bad, generally speaking, and for the most part, the criminals he comes into contact with are unlikely to want to torture and kill him should by chance he fall into their hands. They typically choose to leave an area if possible, not engage in a strong defense much less an offensive attack of the type the military Special Operator may anticipate. The civilian Special Operator, however, must be ready for a mission almost every minute of the day they are on duty, unless engaging in training. Even if training, they know a sudden call out may occur. This lingering knowledge that at any given moment, a call may come and within minutes often they may be engaged in a life-and-death hostage or raid situation, can be very wearing on the individual operator. The knowledge that any action cannot be truly viewed as a success unless the criminal is ultimately convicted, which may not occur due to a variety of factors completely outside the actions of the Special Operator, can make life difficult also. Lastly, and I think quite possibly worse, the civilian operator knows, knows, in the back of his mind, that if things really go bad for any one of a hundred reasons, he is very likely to be thrown to the wolves of the press and local population to save the administrators or political leaders leaving him to lose the position he enjoys as a Special Operator, perhaps his entire career, income/pension loss, often his own assets to a civil judgment, and perhaps end up in jail. It takes someone with a pretty mature, stable mind to confront all of these things and still exercise the necessary judgment to accomplish the intended task. For this reason, the civilian Special Operator is often, but not always, somewhat older than his military counterpart.

Chapter 15   Top guns

The firearms used by a Special Operations man are always an interesting issue. Naturally Special Operations personnel will normally use all the weapons commonly utilized by their nation's military at a given time frame, and they also will use or be familiar with, the weapons that are used by their opponents at the time. Thus a review of Special Operations weapons would include all military types of weapons that are available to any combatants at a given time frame and locality.

However, Special Operators also due to training, skill level, perceived actual needs, and other factors ("neatness" or "coolness" being a big one in many cases) typically use weapons that may not be common in the military inventory of the nation at a given time. After all, what is one of the advantages of being a Special Operator, if it is not the ability to be different, act differently, look different and carry a different weapon?

This perceived need to use special weapons is possibly most marked in hostage/rescue/counterterrorist teams that have become one of the main areas of action for both military and civilian Special Operations. It makes sense in some regards that these special tasks will use different weapons than what a typical line infantryman might find most useful. Accordingly a wide variety of unusual weapons have crept into the Special Operations arsenals around the world. But oddly enough, upon careful examination, it appears a lot of Special Operations hostage/rescue/counterterrorist units today use the same weapons. That may be, of course, due to the fact that certain weapons simply work best for a given task, many teams train with each other thus passing on the idea that a given item is best by actual test or it can be simply a fashion statement. It may also be a little of each. Whatever the reason, a search of open sources that describe the weapons typically used sees some weapons constantly being used with only an occasional oddity creeping in, mostly due to someone in a specific unit liking something possibly or being willing to think "outside the box."

In the paragraphs to follow, I will outline these rather standard weapons that are encountered but I again would like to note that many other weapons are on occasion encountered, that we are dealing with current-day special units involved with hostage/rescue/counterterrorist missions, not general military Special Operations, and that the common weapons used by Special Operations units in days past, today, and in the future will also be the standard infantry weapons used by the nation's infantry forces as well as that used by their enemy opponents.

The submachinegun is almost a standard staple of the Special Operator in this field. Typically standard military men use rifles today and police are armed with handguns. To deploy with a submachinegun at the ready marks the person as someone who is going forth to do imminent battle at close range with a dangerous enemy. Hence the SMG.

In the early days, the short, overall length, post-World War II SMG was the one most commonly encountered. These typically fired from an open bolt position and used a telescoping bolt to allow a relatively long barrel in comparison to the overall length of the weapon. Of course, open-bolt guns worked very well in all sorts of difficult circumstances and for that reason,

Above: Left-side view of a
Micro UZI 9mm SMG
(closed bolt).

Below: The author firing an
MAT 49 SMG.

Left-side view of MAS
M1938 7.65mm SMG.

French police officer in the
1950s searching the
rooftops of Paris for
criminals. He uses an MAS
38 SMG.

Left-side view of Beretta PM12 (S) with the stock folded.

The author with the Beretta PM12 (S) 9x19 mm SMG.

The Walther SMG: top, the MPK, below, the MPL.

The author firing a Beretta PM12 (S) 9 x 19mm SMG.

even in teams that have gone to closed-bolt weapons today, the open-bolt SMG is frequently retained for water-borne missions where activity in the surf zone will soon fill up the weapon with sand. Open-bolt guns with loose tolerances and powerful springs seem to work best in these situations.

Some early teams used the UZI SMG and it is still found in standard, mini and micro versions some places. It is a fine weapon. Remember, the US Secret Service thinks well enough of it to use it to protect the President. It can be shot accurately to make fine shots. Secret Service Agents are known to be capable of shooting flying doves with their UZIs. I have been able to hit flying clays with both standard and micro versions myself. Many lesser-trained shooters find making delicate shots with an open-bolt SMG difficult, however, and have migrated to a closed-bolt gun.

Some national teams have retained their military open-bolt SMG to perform the tasks especially in the early days of the job or as noted when sand penetration is thought to be a problem. The French have used their MAT49 SMG for this reason, the Spaniards their Z-63/70, and the Swedes their M37/9 Suomi SMG. It appears that the British have maintained a supply of their silenced Sterling MK VI SMG for such missions also and originally they used the standard open-bolt MK IV Sterling for the tasks. Other open-bolt guns that are encountered, the Swedish M45, Walther MPL and MPL-K, Ingram M10 and M11 and, of course, the Beretta PM12. The Italians have apparently started to adopt closed-bolt weapons, but I must say this seems more like a desire to adopt an exotic special weapon and to keep in fashion step than any real need, for the PM12 is certainly as good as any SMG made. The Ingram M10/11 SMG were early favorites with lots of teams around the world due to available chamberings in .45 ACP, 9 x 19 and 9 x 17 mm in the case of the M11 but even more likely due to the availability of factory supplied suppressors and short overall length. While the Ingrams all fired way too fast to be truly useful, they were quite handy and the suppressors were really a nice feature especially in the early 1970s when suppressed SMG were quite rare except for old World War II MK IIS and MK VI Stens, and new L34A1 Sterlings.

In the US, early teams used the M3A1 SMG (one of course instantly recalls the Marine Special Operators of the early 1920s in Central America with their M1921/8 Thompson SMG). One of their M3A1s was found at the scene of the disaster in the Iranian desert when Jimmy Carter attempted a raid to rescue US Embassy personnel held captive by "militant students." The M3A1, of course, was not a good SMG to begin with, being heavy and full of sharp edges, but it did have a slow rate of fire allowing easy shot placement and could be readily suppressed. The Colt CAR 15 9 x 19 mm SMG variant of the M16 rifle came into being and has found some success especially with teams that are already using the M16 rifle as the manual of arms is the same which helps with training. A factory suppressed weapon is available which helps in raids to keep noise down both inside the raided structure and outside to keep local neighbors ignorant of the raid. It also helps reduce flash, helpful in those areas where volatile chemicals might exist.

I have always thought the Colt CAR 15 9 x 19 mm SMG really came out to allow teams in the US to buy new SMGs when procurement policies demanded they buy US-made, not foreign, products. These SMGs have had a lot of functioning problems due to a poorly designed magazine housing caused by the failure at the time the weapon came out to buy a proper broach. Hence anyone buying one needs to carefully match the weapon to fully functioning (and tested) magazines and never let them out of their control thereafter as not all magazines will seemingly work in all guns and one seems to be unable to tell exactly why.

The most widely used SMG as of this date (2002) seems to be the Heckler & Koch MP5. This can be in the standard variant with fixed or collapsing stock, the integrally suppressed MP5SD model, or the shortened MP5K model. All of these models typically chamber the 9 x 19 mm cartridge (the .40 S&W models and 10 mm versions are quite rare and certainly have never been utilized by any Special Operations teams that I know of, except for the FBI Hostage Rescue Team utilizing the 10 mm MP5 model). They are patterned on the post-war H&K rifle, the G3. Naturally the barrel is shorter and the overall length and weight less. The weapons all use the roller-lock principle which is, of course, totally unnecessary for the pistol cartridge shot but I guess it allows for high pressure specialty ammunition to be used and it keeps the bolt light while still keeping the cyclic rate low. The weapons, interestingly, do not use a telescoping bolt and thus are long in comparison to some SMGs. The grip is nice and a variety of different trigger systems is available, from safe and semi auto only to safe, single shot and burst to safe, single 2/3 shot burst to full auto burst and a bunch in between. The most useful thing about the MP5 for Special Operations work seems to be the fact that unlike most SMGs, it fires like a rifle with a closed bolt. Thus the jarring release of the bolt felt when the trigger on an open-bolt SMG is fired is missing. This permits the users, especially the less well trained, to correctly place their bullets on a small target at some range and thereby get the pinpoint accuracy often sought in hostage/rescue work. It, of course, fires only the 9 x 19 mm cartridges and since it weights 5½ pounds, it has very little recoil again making it easy and comfortable to shoot. The safety is much handier than that found on many SMGs so it can be deployed faster. Heckler & Koch has developed a good sling system, the weapons are well-made out of good materials, and are reliable. They are rather difficult to clean properly having way too many nooks and crannies, and the barrel being too deep in the receiver for my tastes to be easily cleaned but they are otherwise fine SMGs. Anyone can shoot an MP5 easily and while the expert will notice the jarring effect as the bolt hits the back of the receiver each time it fires, this will not be noticed by the less expert who will find the lack of a jarring bolt release comforting. Also I believe also a lot of people are simply alarmed or at least ill at ease with an open-bolt SMG that will fire simply by closing the bolt. Naturally such concerns, based on unfamiliarity with a weapon design, are a lot like those raised by people to cocked and locked or condition one carry for single action auto loaders but it is a problem and needs to be recognized.

Heckler & Koch must be one of the luckiest gun companies in the world, for their weapons were used by the SAS at Prince's Gate in 1980 in front of the world. Almost overnight, the MP5 became as instantly recognizable as the Colt Single-Action, Luger, Thompson and AK 47. That mission became the standard by which all others could be graded and all the teams in the world wanted to emulate the SAS. So they also got their MP5 SMG. It is a good SMG but it still is only an SMG. As long as proper ammunition is used, and it is not carried in very harsh areas and cleaning is carefully done, it will serve

The author firing the FA MAS from the prone, bipod-supported position. Quite effective work can be done in this manner.

the Special Operator's purposes quite nicely, but it is no death ray or magic wand – it is merely a pistol-powered, short rifle that can fire more than one round with a single pull of the trigger in many situations.

The new FN P90 which uses the unique 5.7 x 28 mm cartridge is like an SMG in many ways and may offer new potential in that area. It is so new that few are out there. A few teams had them but more as an experiment than anything else. A friend related an experience with one on a recent raid that was quite disappointing, I am sorry to say. Too many shots, too many good hits and too few deaths for good taste. Time will tell.

After a number of seasons when the SMG was utilized as the Special Operator's shoulder weapon of choice, it dawned on many that pistol-powered shoulder weapons were really limited by the cartridge power and

The author firing the FA MAS in the off-hand position.

Special Operations: weapons & tactics

The author with the FA MAS in the ready position. the sling allows the weapon's weight to be supported, but it releases quickly to allow the weapon to be fired.

something with more power was needed. Naturally the Special Operator could easily go to his nation's infantry rifles and many of them did so but many of the tasks they were confronted with, a standard infantry rifle was too long and awkward. Many teams are using things such as the Heckler & Koch G3, 33, AUG with 20-inch barrel, Colt M16A1 and M16A2, FNC, AR18, AKM, AK 74, FAL, Beretta M70, Galil, Daewoo K1/K2, and SIG Stg. 90 (550). Commercial semi-auto variants of these are often seen in civilian Special Operations teams and the Ruger Mini-14 is also seen in both semi and burst

The author firing the FA MAS 5.56 x 45mm; note the gas cloud immediately in front of the muzzle in this photograph: this shows the lack of felt recoil, and how quickly the firing position can be resumed – a very handy rifle in the author's experience and a much better weapon than anticipated from reviews.

The author with a Daewoo 5.56 SMG version of the K1. The collapsing stock makes a shorter package than the CAR 15 Colt SMG (XM177E1/20 but it is not as comfortable on the cheek.

fire mode, the latter being developed for the French Police and being one of their special favorites for their Special Operations teams of the police.

Naturally Special Operators soon found out that the "Goldilocks" problem existed with their rifles and SMG. The power level was good with the rifles and the size was nice with the SMG. What was needed was a weapon that combined the rifle power in an SMG package. It would be nice if it did not have a lot of flash and was controllable for second or subsequent shots. Cutting down the standard infantry rifle really did not solve the problem. Every time anyone chops 8 to 14 inches off a 7.62 x 51 mm battle rifle, you are left with a loud, flashy, bright muzzle signature and lose substantial control.

Daewoo 5.56 mm SMG version of the K1; top, left side view, below right side. The stock is similar to the M3 SMG. Note that the bolt handle is very stable, handy for kicking open and pulling to the rear with the left hand, unlike the M16 rifle.

Going to smaller cartridges like the 5.56 x 45 mm and 5.45 x 39 mm helps a lot in terms of control as the light bullets simply recoil less. But they still penetrate ballistic vests better than 9 x 19 mm SMG and generally offer better stopping power.

Some Special Operations groups used Bullpup-type rifles that are standard infantry models. The FA MAS used in the French military is just such a weapon. It has proven quite useful and is a dandy weapon, in my experience. The H&K 53, Colt M4, AUG in 14-inch or 16-inch versions, SIG 551-16 inch or 552-8 inch, Ruger AC556 K, AR18(s) and Galil or South African variants

Comparison of the Heckler & Koch 53 SMG with 8.5" barrel and the AUG with 16" barrel.

(SAR models) are all examples of this breed of .22 caliber rifle with shortened barrels (or short overall lengths) which are based on standard infantry weapons. The M4 is possibly a tad long for optimal use but certainly not impossible and better than its full length counterpart. The same can be said for the SIG 551, Ruger AC556-K, and 13½-inch Galil variants. G36K, the shorter AR 18/180, H&K 53, SIG 552, H&K and AUG, especially in 14-inch due to its bullpup construction. Keeping overall length down, despite the 14-inch barrel, all are very useful. Blast is a bit of a problem but careful ammunition selection, especially in non-military teams, will help minimize flash problems and if the Special Operator learns to use the weapon in a rapid-fire semi-auto mode rather than a burst-fire mode, I believe he will be well satisfied with the results obtained which will be far better than any 9 x 19 mm SMG will render while still giving the operator a package as handy as many SMGs typically seen in Special Operator's hands. While not commonly seen outside the old Soviet Bloc countries, the 5.45 x 39 mm AKSU, except for its slower-to-disengage safety, is also an excellent Special Operations weapon. With ammunition about 10% less powerful than 5.56 x 45 mm, blast and flash are less of a problem and recoil is even more controllable also. The weapon itself is light and lively feeling in your hands and no longer than an MP5. I believe the AKSU is so far superior to the H&K MP5 (or the newly released but to date rarely seen H&K UMP SMG) that there is simply no comparison. It is also substantially cheaper than its nearest competitor, the SIG 552 (which may be out of production currently).

Special Operations: weapons & tactics

The author with a group shot at 50 feet with 40 WMP in two-shot burst mode. Note the climb of holes from the second shot to the right.

The author firing a Benelli Super 90 12 gauge with Federal tactical 12 gauge buckshot loads. The weapon cycles fast and has light recoil, which, coupled with tactical loads allows quick response times, as seen here where the case has just cleared the weapon but the shooter is ready for the next shot already.

The author with two Saiga 20 gauge short-barreled shotguns, one fixed stock and one folding stock model.

I would have thought the day of the SMG was over in 1940 when the US introduced the M1 carbine but due to the rise of terrorism and military-style teams to confront it, the SMG had a bit of a respite but the top teams have now seen the light and moved on to rifle power cartridges fired in weapons the size of many SMG. This effect will no doubt trickle down to the lower level teams over the next 30 years as it always does.

Shotguns have been used by Special Operations units of all types for as long as cartridge shotguns have been around. Certainly they were used by US troops in the Philippines and during World War I; their effectiveness on trench raids and such was clearly evidenced by the Germans' protest over their use and threat of executing US troops caught armed with them. This from the group who brought the world such cultural delights as poison gas and flame throwers! However, oddly enough, shotguns seem to be a weapon only commonly deployed by the United States and occasionally by the British. When the US wanted to equip Vietnamese villagers with shotguns for defensive purposes, they sat, ignored and rusting, in warehouses, the Vietnamese preferring the M1 or M2 carbines and M16 rifles for the task, no doubt a reflection on their French military history (and no doubt also due to the lack of insight that called for 18-inch, full-stocked, 12-gauge shotguns instead of 14-inch, 20-gauge shotguns with shortened butts and soft recoil pads).

Special Operations: weapons & tactics

Mosberg M590 12 gauge shotgun being utilized by a US Military Special Response (SRT) member.

The shotgun in the military has always been a rather ignored relative for the most part, lacking the firepower and penetration of a machinegun, the handiness of a handgun and the accuracy of a rifle at ranges beyond 25 yards. For close ranges under 25 yards typically – occasionally greater range depending on the load and individual weapon – a lot of shotgun patterning seems a bit magical to me – nothing is quite as deadly for the first few shots. After that, things get a lot worse for almost every shotgun seen (with the possible exception of the new Russian Saiga 20-gauge shotgun which uses an AKM receiver) is merely a converted sporting shotgun. They are slow to reload, difficult to maintain, and generally lack effective sights. Finishes can be added to make them more durable in that regard and sights added to allow better shot placement, but they are still hard to maintain in the field and not nearly as sturdy as one normally expects a quality military weapon to be.

On many Special Operation teams today, the shotgun is present to do things like blow locks and hinges off as well as extinguish lights. They are also useful when low penetration is greatly desired and a low non-military appearance is desired for a civilian Special Operation team. For military Special Operation teams operating in a rural environment, I do not believe they are worth the weight to carry unless you go to something like the Saiga 20-gauge. Then you get an effective piece of kit. In urban areas, whether for military or civilian teams, they may have a place but the very real limitations noted must be taken into account.

Teams that are being influenced by US teams (or movies) frequently will adopt shotguns as same as found among their US counterparts. The Mossberg 500 series is a shotgun designed to meet military specifications for strength with a thick barrel to avoid dents and is as rugged as you could hope for in a converted sporting-pattern shotgun. It is best to buy it equipped with rifle peep sights and go with the 14-inch barrel since nothing over that is really needed but typically you see the 18-inch plain bead sight model due to costs. The Ithica M37 has long been a favorite and its downward ejection has always found favor both with left-handed operators as well as those who are concerned about hugging cover. The Remington M870 is an almost standard police shotgun in the US and thus familiar to most Special Operators in the civilian field from earlier experience. It, of course, is a simple weapon for the military operator. Again the 14-inch barrel variant with a peep rear sight and rifle blade front with a rust resistant finish is best but rarely seen due to costs and legal entanglements in the US with shotguns having a barrel under 18 inches. The auto loading Model 11-87 is available in 18-inch barrel length and is a nice shotgun especially as it is an auto loader for those who can be trusted to handle it safely. But it is a mere converted sporting weapon not nearly up to the Saiga 20-gauge standards. All of these US shotguns are found around the world with teams that either are deeply influenced by their US counterparts directly or indirectly and who do not have a domestic source of combat shotguns.

Teams from countries that have a vibrant arms industry, like Belgium, Italy and Germany, who choose to use a shotgun have had their factories modify sporting shotguns for their purposes. Naturally such shotguns suffer the same problems that such converted sporting shotguns come with in the US when the same thing is done. In Europe, it is possibly even worse, however, in that the ones modified are typically auto loaders and much too complex in their modes of operation. The German teams that use the Benelli and Heckler & Koch shotguns must be composed of very smart people as I found the manual of arms necessary to get them into operation so involved as to be silly. The SPAS 12 featured in Italy that can be used as a pump or auto loader with a folding stock that seems to always catch your hand someplace along the load, is likewise way too involved for basic "grunts" like me. I am likewise not happy with the Beretta shotguns that are involved to load, lack decent sights, and have a poor finish. This on top of being a mere converted sporting shotgun with all the problems that brings to the issue.

The Koreans, at their Daewoo plant, have made the selective-fire USAS 12-gauge shotgun which fires from a box or drum. It is rather like an oversized M16 rifle but, of course, fires 12-gauge shotgun shells. I have found it to be an awkward, heavy weapon of little practical use. If scaled down to M16 size, it might have its place but that is unlikely to happen since the US market for semi-auto variants has been closed to it by people who apparently are incapable of reading the US Constitution and its accompanying Bill of Rights. Hopefully that will change in the years ahead and those ignorant, ill-cultured types will be relegated to the dustbins of history where such poor thinkers belong. While the USAS-12 is seen from time to time, I know of no one who really seriously deploys it.

In Russia, the 12- and 20-gauge shotguns based on the AK 47 rifle are seen. They are available in a variety of butt stock styles (fixed and folding) and different barrel lengths. All use detachable box magazines and are based on the well-known, reliable AK 47 action. I view them as the most significant breakthrough in the field of fighting shotguns. While not commonly seen in the hands of Special Operations teams, their main market seeming to be Russian Security guards who apparently can get licenses for shotguns but not handguns (licenses to bear arms apparently being a curious concept acceptable in a formerly totalitarian but still authoritarian state), but I would imagine that they will find their places in more and more Special Operations groups'

Russian soldier in World War II with the M91/30 Mosin Nagent sniper rifle.

armories as they become well known.

The sniper rifle is a very important tool for all Special Operations groups. The ability to reach out and kill someone upon command at a given time who may be far away and possibly threatening danger to people who are standing close by while at the same time avoiding inflicting damages upon innocent people is one of the most commonly imposed tasks a Special Operation group will be given. It is also sometimes one of the most difficult callings for sound judgment, good tactics, excellent marksmanship and a willingness to take another person's life directly and without doubt of a given time. For many people, this is very difficult. For others, it is surprisingly easy although even for them, it sometimes will cause problems down the road. Your team must strike the first group out of the team as they have no business being there as they will create a risk for everyone including themselves. Your second group you want, but a wise leader will take steps to help the individual of all levels so as to not create a disabled soldier or police officer at some distant day.

The sniper rifles that are called for really differ in some regards and are the same in others. What they are not, however, is what some people try to make them. A Special Operations sniper rifle is not a target rifle designed to fire a large number of shots from a given position on a known distance range. It is instead a rifle that will be fired once or twice from a position but will need to deliver the rounds to the same place each time, a rifle that will not lose its zero as it is carried in the field or in a vehicle, a rifle that will shoot accurately at the necessary ranges, and deliver a good blow when the bullet hits the target.

Many sniper rifles designed for Special Operations units are really simply military sniper rifles. Unfortunately most of them also suffer from the identity crisis of thinking themselves to be target rifles, not combat rifles. A military sniper rifle should certainly be capable of hitting a man at 1,000 yards – out to 1,500 yards would be even better, assuming a typical .30 caliber cartridge is being used, not one of the specialty rounds like the 338 Lapua or an anti-material rifle like a 50 Barrett or 12.7/14.5 mm weapon. Those rifles can hit

The author with a
Remington M40 sniper rifle.

individual targets at much greater range depending on the weapon. Most, however, are really not designed for individual targets but material to be destroyed. A missile or radar installation is a typical example that comes to mind. A civilian sniper rifle need not worry itself with such distances, 100 yards will do nicely, but the bullet must be able to put the first shot every time into a target no larger than an egg. Barrels do not have to be heavy or long to do either of these tasks since long strings will not be fired, but they must be bedded properly and the stock itself must not move. The triggers should be crisp and controllable. The scope and mounts must be precise and hold their

Special Operations: weapons & tactics

The author with a Steyr Tactical Scout 308 equipped with 1.5 x 4 Schmidt & Bender scope with a 10-shot magazine installed.

positions. It should be painted to break up in the surroundings so the Special Operator sniper is less likely to be spotted by his enemy. I think the rifle should be short enough and light enough to permit the sniper to carry the rifle without fatigue and to be able to crawl, run or do anything else it takes to get into position without exhausting himself.

One of the key concerns here is whether to use a semi-automatic rifle which, of course, allows a more rapid repeat shot or to select a bolt-action weapon which, at the high end, will typically be more accurate than an equal quality self loader and also typically be a lot cheaper to produce and easier to maintain. The other issues involve cartridge selection. The battle there seems to be between selecting a full power rifle round like the 7.62 x 51 mm or 7.62 x 54 R or to go to the new .22 caliber cartridges being used. Obviously the first pick has a lot of good quality ammunition already worked up for it and will send a bullet down range easily but the smaller cartridge has now proven its ability to buck the wind if proper load is used and can certainly be deadly.

The semi-automatic sniper rifle seems to be centered around variants of the Heckler & Koch G3 as fitted up for sniper use. This can vary depending upon the level required as between an STG-1 which is a very basic semi-auto sniping rifle to the incredibly expensive PSG-1. Frankly, I find most H&K triggers to be terrible, even the best is not great, and it has proven to be very difficult to get a good solid mount on sheet-metal receivers found on those rifles. Good performance can be had but at great expense and effort that, in my opinion, would be better spent on spare ammunition and more training. In the US, the sniper variant of the M14 called the M21 was used in the Vietnam

War, and these weapons were well regarded and found to do a good job. Unfortunately the sniper version of the M14 rifle is a difficult weapon to maintain if the accuracy is to be retained at the highest level. Some Special Operations units have access to a full-time armorer and if you do also, then the rifle is an excellent choice. The other semi-players in this .30 caliber semi-auto sniper rifle field seem to be the AR-10 which is only rarely seen by teams but I understand has become common in Israel in the last few years, the Galil 7.62 sniper variant and the Soviet designed SVD sniper unit now made in other countries. The latter rifle seems to be a little on the low end for performance beyond 600 meters but I suppose good work could be done with it, especially at the shorter engagement distances. The scope it has on it is a bit cluttered to me and seems difficult to use quickly. The Galil sniper really does not seem to me to be a dedicated sniper unit and I would have to see groups at say 600 to800 yards before I could agree that it is really a first-class sniper rifle. The AR-10 falls into the same category, in my opinion.

A wide variety of bolt-action sniper rifles is used by current civilian and military Special Operations units. Interestingly, the civilian unit often copies from the gear used by the military unit which, of course, is a bad idea for they actually are using weapons that are not truly suited for their tasks and when these same weapons are then used by civilian teams, they are even more ill suited to the actual real-world tasks. Most of these rifles come in a bolt-action format with a medium-heavy barrel of 24 to 26 inches. By the time they add everything on, they will weigh 12 or more pounds typically up to the totally unnecessary 18½ pounds for the Marine Corps. sniping rifle – the M40A3.

The Germans have used their Mauser manufactured bolt-action Mauser 66 SP but seem to really prefer their incredibly expensive H&K rifles. I believe it is the German belief in high tech that has caused this selection more than anything else. The Belgian teams often sport the FN sniper rifles which originally were based on Mauser M98 actions and now use actions very similar to pre-64 Winchester M70 actions. The French teams and those who are trained by them seem to favor their domestically-made FR-F1 which, of course, uses a receiver designed to be like the MAS 36 which is really quite a nice rifle although the lack of safety bothers many. Swiss teams and others who like high-end equipment will be found with the SSG 3000 rifles and, of course, many will still be found with Steyr SSG rifles.

The British have brought their Accuracy International rifle to the Special Operations world and, due to the big impact British teams have had on this field, this rifle has had a lot more use than its true qualities would merit. It is, if anything, the perfect example of the wrong features being adopted. Malcolm Cooper designed the rifle and he was an excellent target shooter. He died in 2001. When he set out to build a sniper rifle, he took many of those features and put them on his weapon. It resulted in a heavy, awkward, dead-feeling weapon that is a good shooting rifle but not a very useful sniper rifle for the military. It is definitely a bad one for the civilian operator due to the location of the safety, which requires the shooter to either leave it off when in position so a quick shot can be taken (with all the danger that it possesses) or break your grip when ready to shoot to either close the bolt (assuming the safety is not engaged) or flip it off which, of course, takes time and may cause the civilian Special Operator who is waiting for the instant to make the shot to miss the opportunity. I guess the British liked it in light of their old Enfield

Left-side view of the Heckler & Koch USP 9 x 19mm.

L42 rifles they had been hauling around for so long, but really it is hardly satisfactory. Still, it is widely used around the world.

In the United States and elsewhere, unless the country has a vibrant arms industry capable of making sniper rifles, the standard is almost always a Remington M700-based weapon.

It is in the area of handguns that Special Operators really are different than traditional military units as far as equipment for, while every military Special Operator carries a handgun almost without exception, it is a rare thing in traditional military units unfortunately. Rather like in civilian Special Operations units, all members typically carry a shoulder weapon in addition to a handgun unlike the normal policeman who rarely deploys with a shoulder weapon.

As noted earlier in military Special Operations, the type of handgun typically encountered is probably not entirely well thought-of among many groups for it is unlikely to get much use and the size and weight occupied by the handgun would likely be better served carrying extra ammunition, grenades or water, but in the hostage/rescue/counterterrorist mode, the handgun, whether we are talking about civil or military teams, really comes into its own.

Of course, since many teams come from a military background, it is not at all surprising that the military-issued handgun is carried. Sometimes it is specially modified to make it more accurate and easier to shoot accurately.

Left-side view of the Beretta M9 9 x 19 mm.

This is certainly the case in US military teams when the M1911A1 pistol, which has had such a fine history of gun fighting, is still clung to by some. The specially modified M1911A1 pistols are an issue item for the SWAT Team and a commercial high capacity variant, the Para Ordnance P14 as modified by Les Bauer, is the signature gun of the FBI's HRT (Hostage Rescue Team) having replaced the 9 mm P35 (Hi-Power) pistols originally carried. Frankly I have some doubts about the usefulness of .45 ACP pistols today given the common usage of body armor and web gear filled with steel magazines full of steel-cased ammunition worn on the chest is the Chicom fashion but the pistols themselves are often fine examples. They do get shot a lot and keeping them up and running has proven to be a real maintenance problem as the highly-refined M1911A1-style pistol is rather like a race horse not a plow horse, I fear. But if you have the maintenance facilities, they are a good piece of kit.

Others on the US teams at both civil and military levels are found to use common military-type pistols of known reliability in 9 x 19 mm. These include the Glock 17, Beretta (both standard M9 and the "G" Version), the SIG P226 and P228 and P35 (Hi-Power) pistols are common. Of course, such weapons are also common throughout the world for they are well regarded by almost everyone although the SIG and Beretta are perhaps a bit wide in the butt and slide for some purposes. Some US teams also utilize standard duty weapons like the S&W M5906 (and variants) that are patrol division issue to get the maximum amount of familiarity with their weapons. In Europe, interestingly

Special Operations: weapons & tactics

SIG P228 with 50 yards group shot by the author off hand with Federal +P+ 115 gr. ammo.

enough, revolvers are sometimes seen especially in the French teams and those influenced by them. The Manhurin MR 73 was the signature weapon for the French GIGN and Austria Cobra Units and a finer .357 Magnum revolver could not be wanted. Early German teams were commonly seen with Smith & Wesson M28, M36, M19 (2½ inches), M49 and M13 revolvers. Most Special Operations groups have decided to go to a higher capacity weapon, however, so the revolver is not the common weapon although in all honesty it is likely to do just fine for the real-world work needed.

Double-column auto loaders in 9 x 19 mm seem to be very popular and, depending on national origin, some pistols not commonly seen in police or military work are encountered due to either nationalistic pride for possession or more likely an inability to convince the "bean counters" to release foreign exchange to buy other non-national products. This is the case, no doubt, with

the Israeli use of the Jericho 941, the French involvement with the MAB PA 15 and the Czech (and some other areas where their weapons sell at very attractive prices in comparison to Western European products) use of the CZ75 and CZ85. This also explains the South African use of the M88 (a Beretta M92 copy) and its variants.

Some countries that are just gearing up and have little firearms real-world-related experience for their military or police Special Operations groups to act upon will take military weapons from the arsenals and use them for the teams. This explains things like the Polish use of the P-64 and

Left-side view of the Heckler & Koch M23 pistol: it is a large pistol.

Left-side view of the Beretta M93R with the stock extended and the selector set on burst fire mode.

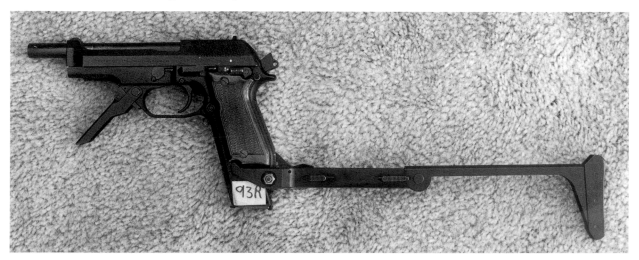

The author with the Stechkin machine pistol with stock attached – quite effective.

PM 63 and the Egyptian use of the Helwan copy of the Beretta M951.

Heckler & Koch has been in the forefront of weapons designed for Special Operations teams over the years. Their P9 is a little elderly now although it can be easily equipped with a suppressor, and, owing to its sights and the locking system, will still function properly when others will not. The US Navy

The author with a group fired from a Glock G18 on burst fire shot at five yards, two-shot bursts used. The first round hit in the low center and the second hit in the throat/head region.

SEALs are known users of this design and it is really quite handy, I have found in my shooting tests. The P7 is an advanced design favored by some German State Police Forces and has found its way into Special Operations groups also. I find it to be heavy for its cartridge and of low capacity in light of such things as the Glock 17/9 but those who like it swear by it. I believe it is a unique design and if used by a person, they probably should limit themselves to that one pistol and not switch around. Rather like a triggerless Colt SAA slip gun in that regard, I suppose. As a chronic tester and gun swapper, I found I could not feel comfortable with it. Heckler & Koch has developed a series of polymer high-capacity pistols that are quite useful for Special Operations due to their reliability and low maintenance. The USP in a variety of trigger/safety modes is certainly reliable although too wide across the slide for me. Their

Special Operations: weapons & tactics

Above: The author firing a Stechkin machine pistol without a stock; note that the selector is in semi mode.

Below: Left side view of Yugoslavian copy of VZ61 7.65mm SMG with stock extended.

Tactical Model of this pistol comes with a barrel already threaded for a suppressor and it is thus handy although you need to watch the suppressor used due to the recoil action used to function the pistol. The roller-lock design on the P9 avoided this problem. Both of these weapons are available in 9 x 19 mm and .45 ACP, if for some reason you prefer that cartridge, although it is hard to see why you would for Special Operations work (and I like .45 pistols!). Of course, the star of the H&K line-up for Special Operations use is their MK 23. This pistol was designed specifically to meet the demands of the US Navy SEALs. Like all H&K pistols, it is accurate and reliable but also way too wide in the slide and butt to be a very useful belt gun, in my opinion. Any weapon that big should come with a stock in my opinion, but some people seem to like it. Perhaps they simply do not know better or like the cachet it brings with it.

While most of the handguns selected for Special Operations are semi-automatic, a few seen offer the benefit of burst firing. A machine pistol in capable hands is probably the single most deadly hand-held weapon in the world at five yards and under, in my opinion. It takes a lot of practice to get good using them and at least a 1,000 pounds a month thereafter in a proper course of fire to stay good but for someone who seeks the best weapon for close combat, drug raids and searches, it is the answer. The Glock M18 is simply a wonderful weapon in this regard. The Soviet Stechkin is also an excellent piece within the limits of its ammunition which, of course, is of

Author firing Yugoslavian version of VZ61 SMG. Note that the bolt to the rear and the case are in the air in this photograph yet the muzzle is level, showing the low recoil.

lower power and fewer variations than what is available for the 9 x 19 mm chambered Glock M18. The Czech-based Skorpian has some followers.

Some new weapons have come on the scene in the last several years and we can expect to see more of them in the future. The .40 S&W cartridge has developed a following in US Police circles in the last several years and I would anticipate we will see more handguns and possibly SMGs in that chambering in the years ahead in civilian Special Operations teams. Of course, the pistols themselves, typically Beretta M96, Glock 22/23, and SIG P226/9 are already weapons familiar to all by virtue of their 9 mm counterparts. I do not anticipate seeing such a cartridge being injected into military teams just because of the problem of ammunition resupply. I would anticipate teams picking .40 S&W SMGs in the future also if they are going to select such a style of weapon. Of course, a short-barrel rifle-cartridge-firing weapon is likely better such as the AKSU, SIG 552 or FA MAS but if you re going to have an SMG in a unit with .40 S&W pistols, then you might as well get a .40 UMP (a .45 UMP in units with .45 pistols, of course) and thereby avoid the problem of getting 9 mm ammunition into .40 S&W weapons which can happen creating problems arranging from malfunctions and not firing to blowing it up completely.

More interesting yet is the likelihood of new cartridges like the 5.7 x 28 mm mentioned earlier chambered in the SMG-like P90 or handgun, the FN Five-seveN. The latter is an especially good weapon offering the ability to penetrate ballistic vests while still not engaging in either excessive ranging or penetration on soft targets. While it is too early to say for sure, such loads may well be the wave of the future especially in either the smallest agency teams of real advanced thinkers or the highest speed national teams where costs are not a concern. In between, it is probably too much cost and too radical a solution until the others lead the way and prove it works. Time will tell.

For those who are interested in evaluation in full involving any of the weapons I have mentioned earlier (and many others besides), evaluations on the item's potential as a weapon of combat, not engineering project, collector qualities or use as a target puncher, I would direct them to my series of books published by Paladin Press which is probably unique in the field of firearms books as being true weapons test and evaluation formats. You can read there about the various weapons, compare them to something you will know which is also evaluated, and then be able to tell for yourself what the strong and weak points are on the various weapons:

1 *The 100 Greatest Combat Handguns (Military Handguns 1870–1995)*
2 *Testing the War Weapons – Infantry Rifles (1870–2000)*: over 160 rifles tested
3 *The Complete Fighting Submachine Gun, Shotgun, and Machine Pistol* over 80 individual weapons evaluated

Special Operations in the 21st century

Chapter 16

I write these lines as we go into the last several weeks of the second year of the 21st century. In the aftermath of the terrorist attacks on September 11, 2001, in the United States, "Special Operations" activities are all the rage. I am constantly coming across articles about how the US and its allies will use their Special Operators "to win the war against terrorism." As an old-time infantry officer and weapons trainer for a variety of Special Operations-type groups and having worked with people from a number of the best Special Operations groups in the world, I am somewhat doubtful. It seems to me that wars are won by men on the ground who take and hold territory. This requires the development of the ultimate weapon – typically the 19-year-old infantryman with a rifle.

A Special Operator can be very useful to conduct short-duration raids, to seize individuals or destroy targets. They can be very helpful in gathering intelligence. They may seize key facilities to deny their use in the enemy or to allow your forces to utilize them, but given the shortage of true Special Operations people, it seems unwise to expect them to operate in the traditional, heavy infantry role. They are neither equipped for the task nor are they trained for it. While they may very well be trained in a variety of interesting and useful tasks, training people to seize and hold terrain in the face of a determined foe and to slug it out with them is not one of those skills.

I believe the future of the battlefields will find a place for bodies of fast-moving, highly skilled individuals who can go in and seize people and objects and destroy selected human as well as material targets, then return to their own position before "a world of hurt" befalls them. We have needed such people always in warfare and there is no reason to believe that the future will be any different but they will never substitute for traditional infantry. The SAS and Long Range Desert Reconnaissance Group in North Africa did excellent work, way out of proportion to the men they had and the resources they used but they could not substitute for the Eighth Army.

On the civilian side of the issue, the militarization of civil police forces is a trend to be deplored, I believe. It has led to a number of unfortunate tragedies in the US at least which have in many ways destroyed excellent reputations enjoyed by agencies prior to that time. A civilian Special Operation group is merely supplied and trained to a higher standard to undertake tasks that could be undertaken by the traditional police units but which, if done, might well expose both them and the general public to greater physical risks. Civilian Special Operators must be very careful not to start thinking of themselves as military men enforcing fiats in an occupied country. If they do so, they will lose the support of the population which in Western countries at least is what has allowed the police to be such a small portion of the population in years past.

The civilian Special Operator must always realize first and foremost that he is a civilian whose job it is to keep the peace by enforcing the law which has been commonly agreed to subject to strict limitations on the ability of government to enforce those laws both as to extent and method in most countries. He must realize that his first and foremost duty is to respect the law and the limitations it imposes on his activities and then after that to attempt to arrest the criminals involved so they can be subject to legal process which is something that is not within his control. If they do that, the population will not shun them, as occurs in many places, as being agents of an oppressive regime and they will not need to hide their faces and conceal their identity. If they conduct themselves properly and respect those who employ them, they have nothing to fear. If they exceed their authority and oppress those who employ them, then it is natural I suppose that they should seek to hide their identity in the hope that retribution will not befall them.

Recommended reading

Any work such as this reflects ideas and thoughts of countless others who have explored the issues over the years. In the case of *Special Operations*, dealing as it does both with the weapons themselves and ammunition as well as how to conduct training to make those who use them the most effective, we can look not only at tactical books but also at firearms books of many types to help us improve our selection of equipment and training.

On the list that follows are books that I have read over the years that deal with the subject at hand which have assisted me in formulating my approach to this subject. You, the reader, can also gain by reading these same books as well as the hundreds of very excellent magazine articles that have appeared on the subject starting as early as the 1870s, in my researches. No one person can possibly try every weapon or training method, but by reading of the experiences of others and evaluating their input in light of your own training and experience, you will learn something useful if you approach the subject with both an open mind as well as an educated one. My test for a good book or article is whether I learned something from reading it that was useful. All of the books that follow have met that test for me and no doubt will for you also.

Suggested reading

Adams, Ronald J, Thomas M McTernan and Charles Remsberg *Street Survival Tactics for Armed Encounters*. Evanston, IL: Calibre Press. 1980.

Applegate, Col. Rex and Michael Janich *Bullseyes Don't Shoot Back*. Boulder, CO: Paladin Press. 1998.

Applegate, Col. Rex and Maj. Chuck Melson *The Close Combat Files of Colonel Rex Applegate*. Boulder, CO: Paladin Press. 1998.

Applegate, Col. Rex. *Combat Use of the Double-Edged Fighting Knife*. Boulder, CO: Paladin Press. 1993.

Applegate, Lt. Col. Rex *Kill – or Get Killed*. Harrisburg, PA: The Military Service Publishing Co. 1951.

Applegate, Rex *Riot Control – Material and Techniques*. Harrisburg, PA: Stackpole Books. 1969.

Askins, Col. Charles *Gunfighters*. Washington, DC: National Rifle Association. 1981.

Askins, Lt. Col. Charles *The Pistol Shooter's Book*. Harrisburg, PA: Stackpole Company. 1 1953.

Aujourd'hui *La Gendarmerie*. Paris, FR: Editions Atlas. 1991.

Avery, Ralph *Combat Loads for the Sniper Rifle*. Cornville, AZ: Desert Publications. 1981.

Ayoob, Massad *Fundamentals of Modern Police Impact Weapons*. Concord, NH: Police Bookshelf. 1984.

Ayoob, Massad *In the Gravest Extreme The Role of the Firearm in Personal Protection*. Self published; no date.

Ayoob, Massad *The Semiautomatic Pistol in Police Service and Self-Defense*. Concord, NH: Police Bookshelf. 1987

Ayoob, Massad *StressFire Volume I of Gunfighting for Police: Advanced Tactics and Techniques*. Concord, NH: Police Bookshelf 1984.

Ayoob, Massad *StressFire II Volume II of Gunfighting for Police: Advanced Tactics and Techniques*. Concord, NH: Police Bookshelf. 1992.

Ayoob, Massad *The Truth About Self Protection*. New York, NY: Bantam Books. 1983.

Baughman, T. Frank *The ABC of Practical Riot Gun Instruction*. Washington, DC: National Rifle Association. 1942.

Bishop, Chris and Ian Drury *Combat Guns. An illustrated encyclopedia of 20th Century Firearms*. Secaucus, NJ: Chartwell Books Inc. 1987.

Bloom, Pete *Practical Rifle Marksmanship*. Exeter, UK: P.J. Bloom. 1993

Blunt, Capt. Stanhope *Rifle and Carbine Firing*. New York, NY: Charles Scribner's Sons. 1995.

Boger, Jan *Combat-Training für den Ernstfall*. Stuttgart, GER: Motobuch-Verlag Stuttgart. 1986.

Boger, Jan *Combat Waffen Combat Schiessen Combat Taktik*. Stuttgart, GER. Motorbuch-Verlag Stuttgart. 1979.

Brennan, Dave *Precision Shooting at 1,000 Yards*. Manchester, CT: Precision Shooting Inc. 2000.

Buttler, W W *The Armed Option Zen in the Art of Combat Pistolcraft*. Sharon Center, OH: Alpha Publications. 1993.

Canfield, Bruce N *A Collector's Guide to United States Combat Shotguns*. Lincoln, RI: Andrew Mowbray. 1992.

Cassidy, William L *Quick or Dead*. Boulder, CO: Paladin Press. 1978.

Chandler, N A and Roy Chandler *Death From Afar*

Volume I. St Mary's City, MD: Iron Brigade Armory. 1992.

Chandler, N A and Roy Chandler *Death From Afar Volume II.* St Mary's City, MD: Iron Brigade Armory. 1993.

Chandler, N A and Roy Chandler *Death From Afar Volume III.* St Mary's City, MD: Iron Brigade Armory. 1994.

Chandler, N A and Roy Chandler *Death From Afar Volume IV.* St Mary's City, MD: Iron Brigade Armory. 1996.

Chandler, N A and Roy Chandler *Death From Afar Volume V.* St Mary's City, MD: Iron Brigade Armory. 1998.

Cheek, John Charles and Tony Lesce *Plainclothes and Off-Duty Officer Survival.* Springfield, IL: Charles Thomas Publisher. 1988.

Crawford, Steve *The SAS at Close Quarters.* London, UK: Sidgwick & Jackson. 1993.

Cirillo, Jim *Guns, Bullets, and Gunfights: Lessons and Tales from a Modern-Day Gunfighter.* Boulder CO: Paladin Press. 1996.

Clede, Bill *Police Handgun Manual: How to Get Street-Smart Survival Habits.* Harrisburg, PA: Stackpole Books. 1985.

Cooper, Jeff *The Art of the Rifle.* Boulder, CO: Paladin Press. 1997.

Cooper, Jeff *The Complete Book of Modern Handgunning.* New York, NY: Bramhall House. 1961.

Cooper, Jeff *Cooper on Handguns.* Los Angeles, CA: Peterson Publishing CO. 1974.

Crossman, Capt. Edward C *Military and Sporting Rifle Shooting.* Onslow, NC: Small-Arms Technical Publishing Co. 1932.

Cutshaw, Charlie *The New World of Russian Small Arms & Ammo.* Boulder, CO: Paladin Press. 1998.

Dockery, Kevin *Special Warfare Special Weapons. The Arms and Equipment of the UDT and Seals from 1943 to the Present.* Chicago, IL: Emperor's Press. no date.

Dove, Patrick Edward *The Revolver Its Description, Management and Use.* Houston, TX: Deep River Armory Inc. Reprint. 1858.

Edwards, Major T J *The Service Rifle and How to Use it. Short Rifle Magazine Lee-Enfield Mark III.* London, UK: Aldershot, Gale & Polden Ltd. Reprint. 1998.

Ezell, Edward Clinton *Small Arms Today.* Harrisburg, PA: Stackpole Books. 1984.

Ezell, Edward Clinton *Small Arms Today.* Harrisburg, PA: Stackpole Books. 2nd Edition. 1988.

Fairbairn, Capt. W E *Get Tough! How to Win in Hand to Hand Fighting.* Boulder, CO: Paladin Press. 1942.

Fairbairn, W E *Shanghai Municipal Police Instructions and Conditions of Practice for the A5 "Colt" Automatic Pistol.* San Francisco, CA: Interservice Publishing Co., Inc. 1981.

Fairbairn, Capt. W E and Captain Eric Anthony Sykes *Shooting to Live with the One-Hand Gun.* Boulder, CO: Paladin Press. 1942.

Farnam, John S *The Farnam Method of Defensive Handgunning.* Kirkland, WA: Firearms Academy of Seattle, Inc. 1994.

Farnam, John *The Street Smart Gun Book.* Concord, NH: Police Bookshelf. 1986.

Felter, Brian A *Police Defensive Handgun Use and Encounter Tactics.* Englewood Cliffs, NJ: Prentice Hall Inc. 1988

Felter, Brian A *Police Shotguns and Carbines.* Englewood Cliffs, NJ: Prentice Hall Inc. 1991.

Firsoff, V A *Ski Track on the Battlefield.* New York, NY: A.S. Barnes and Company. 1943.

Fitzgerald, J H *Shooting.* Hartford, CT: The G. F. Book Company. 1930.

Ford, Roger *The World's Great Machine Guns from 1860 to the Present Day.* London, UK: Brown Packaging Books Ltd. 1999.

Gander, Terry J (ed.) *Jane's Infantry Weapons Twenty-Fifth Edition 1999–2000.* Surrey, UK: Jane's Information Group Inc. 1999.

Gagueche, Yvon *GIGN 10 Ans D'Action.* Paris, FR: Berger Levrault. 1985.

Gaylord, Chic *Handgunner's Guide Including the Art of the Quick-Draw and Combat Shooting.* New York, NY: Hastings House. 1960.

Geller, William A and Michael S Scott *Deadly Force: What We Know.* Washington, DC: Police Executive Research Forum. 1992.

George, J B *Shots Fired in Anger.* Plantersville, SC: Small Arms Technical Publishing Company. 1947.

Geraghty, Tony *The Bullet Catchers Bodyguards and the World of Close Protection.* London, UK: Grafton Books. 1988

Gray, Jim, Mark Monday, and Gary Stubblefield *Maritime Terror Protecting Yourself, Your Vessel, and Your Crew against Piracy.* Boulder, CO: Sycamore Island Books. 1999.

Greener, W W *Sharpshooting for Sport and War.* Prescott, AZ: London 1900.

Greenwood, Supt. Colin *Police Tactics in Armed Operations.* Boulder, CO: Paladin Press. 1979.

Haven, Charles T A *Comprehensive Small Arms Manual.* New York, NY: William Morrow & Co. 1943.

Hogg, Ian V and John Weeks (eds) *Military Small Arms of the 20th Century 6th Edition*. Northbrook, IL: DBI Books. no date.

Hubner, Siegfried F *Combat Shcief & Technik*. Schwend, GER: Journal-Verlag. 1971.

Hubner, Siegfried F *Der erste Treffer zahlt*. Schwend, GER: Journal-Verlag. 1968.

Hubner, Siegfried F *Waffen-Technik*. Schwend, GER: Journal-Verlag. 1974.

Ingersoll, Ralph *The Battle is the Pay-Off*. New York, NY: H. Wolff. 1943.

Jennings, Mike *Instinct Shooting*. Revised Edition. New York, NY: Dodd Meade & Co. 1959.

Johnson, M M *Practical Marksmanship The Technique of Field Firing*. New York, NY: William Morrow & Co. 1945.

Jordan, Bill *No Second Place Winner*. Shreveport, LA: W. H. Jordan. 1965.

Katz, Samuel *Illustrated Guide to the World's Top Counter-Terrorist Forces*. Hong Kong: Concord Publications Co. 1995.

Keith, Elmer *Sixguns*. Harrisburg, PA: The Stackpole Co. 1955.

Keith, Elmer *Sixgun Cartridges and Loads*. Plantersville, SC: Small-Arms Technical Publishing Co. 1936.

Klein, Chuck *Instinct Combat Shooting Defensive Handgunning for Police*. Self Published. 1986

Lau, Mike *The Military and Police Sniper*. Manchester, Ct: Precision Shooting Inc. 1998.

Lauck, Dave *Practical Pistol A Guide Book for Self-Defense and Practical Combat/Competition Shooting*. Gillette, WY: D & L Sports. 1990.

Law, Richard and Peter Brookesmith *The Fighting Handgun. An Illustrated History from the Flintlock to Automatic Weapons*. London, UK: Arms & Armour Press. 1996.

Lee, Kenneth *Big Game Hunting and Marksmanship*. Harrisburg, PA: Telegraph Press. 1941.

Lesce, Tony *Shootout*. Cornville, AZ: Desert Publications. 1979.

Lesce, Tony *Shootout II*. Cornville, AZ: Desert Publications. 1981.

Lesce, Tony *The Shotgun in Combat*. Cornville, AZ: Desert Publications. 1979.

Lewis, Jac and David E Steele. *The Gun Digest Book of Assault Weapons*.Iola, WI: Krause Publications. 2000.

Lind, Ernie *The Complete Book of Trick & Fancy Shooting*. New York, NY: Manchester Press. 1972.

Lipman, Aron *Training Secrets and Techniques of the Master Firearms Instructors*. Self Published. 1993.

Lonsdale, Mark V *Advanced Weapons Training for Hostage Rescue Teams*. Los Angeles, CA: Self Published. 1988.

Lonsdale, Mark V *Bodyguard A Practical Guide to VIP Protection*. Los Angeles, CA: Self Published. 1995.

Lonsdale, Mark V *CQB A Guide to Unarmed Combat and Close Quarter Shooting*. Los Angeles, CA: Self Published. 1991.

Lonsdale, Mark V *Raids A tactical Guide to High Risk Warrant Service*. Los Angeles, CA: Self Published. 1991.

Lonsdale, Mark V *SRT Diver*. Los Angeles, CA: Self Published. 1991.

Lonsdale, Mark V *Sniper II*. Los Angeles, CA: Self Published. 1992.

Lugs, Jaroslav *A History of Shooting Marksmanship, duelling and exhibition shooting*. Middlesex, UK: Spring Books. 1968.

Marshall, Evan P and Edwin J Sanow *Handgun Stopping The Definitive Study Power*. Boulder, CO: Paladin Press. 1992.

Marshall, Evan P and Edwin J Sanow *Stopping Power A Practical Analysis of the Latest Handgun Ammunition*. Boulder, CO: Paladin Press. 2001.

Marshall, Evan P and Edwin J Sanow *Street Stoppers The Latest Handgun Stopping Power Street Results*. Boulder, CO: Paladin Press. 1996.

Mason, James D *Combat Handgun Shooting*. Springfield, IL: Charles C. Thomas. 1976.

McBride, Herbert W *The Emma Gees*. Indianapolis, IN: The Bobbs Merrill Co. 1918.

McBride, Herbert W *A Rifleman Went to War*. Onslow, NC: Small Arms Technical Publishing Co. 1935.

McGivern, Ed *Ed McGivern's Book on Fast and Fancy Revolver Shooting and Police Training*. Springfield, MA: The King-Richardson Co. 1938.

Micheletti, Eric *French Special Forces*. Paris, FR: Histoire & Collections. 1999.

Micheletti, Eric *Le GIGN En Action*. Paris, FR: Histoire & Collections. 1995.

Moyer, Frank and Robert J Scroggie. *Special Forces Combat Firing Techniques*. Boulder, CO: Paladin Press. 1971.

Mroz, Ralph *Defensive Shooting for Real-Live Encounters*. Boulder, CO: Paladin Press. 2000.

Mullin, Timothy J *100 Greatest Combat Pistols Hands-On Test and Evaluations of Handguns from Around the World*. Boulder, CO: Paladin Press. 1994.

Mullin, Timothy J *The Fighting Submachine Gun, Machine Pistol, and Shotgun A Hands-On Evaluation*. Boulder, CO: Paladin Press. 1999.

Mullin, Timothy J *Handbook for Handguns A Comprehensive Evaluation of Military, Police, Sporting and Personal-Defense Pistols*. Boulder, CO: Paladin Press. 2001.

Special Operations: weapons & tactics

Mullin, Timothy J *Testing the War Weapons Rifles and Light Machine Guns from Around the World.* Boulder, CO: Paladin Press. 1997.

Mullin, Timothy J *Training the Gunfighter.* Boulder, CO: Paladin Press. 1981.

Musgrave, Daniel D and Thomas B Nelson *The World's Assault Rifles and Automatic Carbines.* Washington, DC: The Goetz Company. 1967.

Nelson, Thomas and Daniel D Musgrave *The World's Machine Pistols and Submachine Guns Volume II.* Culpeper, VA: Culpeper Publishers. 1980

Nelson, Thomas B and Hans B Lockhoven *The World's Submachine Guns (Machine Pistols) Volume I.* Cologne, GER: International Small Arms. Publishers. 1963.

Noel, J B L *The Automatic Pistol.* London, UK: Foster Groom & Co. Ltd. 1919.

Noel, J B L *How to Shoot with a Revolver.* London, UK: Self published. 1940.

O'Connor, Jack, Roy Dunlap, Alex Kerr, and Jeff Cooper *Complete Book of Shooting.* New York, NY: Harper & Row. 1965.

Paddock, Alfred H U S *Army Special Warfare Its Origins.* Washington, DC: National Defense University Press. 1982.

Peters, Carroll E *Defensive Handgun Effectiveness.* Manchester, TN: Self Published. 1977.

Plaster, John L *SOG A Photo History of the Secret Wars.* Boulder, CO: Paladin Press. 2000.

Pollard, Capt. Hugh B C *Automatic Pistols.* Old Greewich, CT: W E Inc. 1921.

Pollard, Capt. Hugh B C *The Book of the Pistol and Revolver.* London, UK: McBride Nast & Co. Ltd. 1917.

Rauch, Walt *Real-World Survival! What Has Worked for Me.* Lafayette Hill, PA: Rauch & Co. Ltd. 1998.

Reichenbach, William *Automatic Pistol Marksmanship.* Onslow County, NC: Small Arms Technical Publishing CO. 1937.

Reichenbach, William *Six Guns and Bullseyes.* Plantersville SC: Small Arms Technical Publishing CO. 1936.

Remsberg, Charles *The Tactical Edge Surviving High-Risk Patrol.* Northbrook, IL Calibre Press. 1986.

Remsberg, Charles *Tactics for Criminal Patrol Vehicle Stops, Drug Discovery & Officer Survival.* Northbrook, IL Calibre Press. 1995.

Rodgers, Walter R *Huntin' Gun Men – Gun Feel – and Game.* Washington, DC: Infantry Journal Press. 1949.

Rigg, Col. Robert B *Realistic Combat Training and How to Conduct It.* Harrisburg, PA: Military Service Publishing CO. 1955.

Roberts, Duke and Allen P Bristow *An Introduction to Modern Police Firearms.* Beverly Hills, CA: Glencoe Press. 1969.

Robinson, Capt. E H *The Pistol in War Training with Revolver and Self-Loading Pistol.* Aldershot, UK: Gale & Polden Ltd. 1941.

Robinson, Mike *Fighting Skills of the SAS.* London, UK: Sidgwick & Jackson Ltd. 1991.

Robinson, Roger H *The Police Shotgun Manual.* Springfield, IL: Charles C. Thomas. 1973.

Roper, Walter F *Experiments of a Handgunner.* Prescott, AZ: Wolfe Publishing Co. 1989.

Roper, Walter F *Pistol and Revolver Shooting.* New York, NY: MacMillan Company. 1945.

Senich, Peter R *The Long-Range War Sniping in Vietnam.* Boulder, CO: Paladin Press. 1994.

Skocho, Leonard W and Harry A *Greveris. Silencers Patterns and Principles.* Wickenburg, AZ: Normount Technical Publications. 1968.

Smith, W H B *Basic Manual of Military Small Arms.* Harrisburg, PA: Telegraph Press. 1943.

Stafford, David *Camp X OSS, "Intrepid,: and the Allies' North American Training Camp for Secret Agents. c.1941–1945.* New York, NY: Dodd Meade & Co. 1987.

Storm, Barry *Practical Pistoleering A Manual of Practical Revolver Shooting Techniques.* Aguila, AZ: Southwestern Press. 1943.

Suarez, Gabriel *The Tactical Advantage A Definitive Study of Personal Small-Arms Tactics.* Boulder, CO: Paladin Press. 1998.

Suarez, Gabriel *The Tactical Pistol Advanced Gunfighting Concepts and Techniques.* Boulder, CO: Paladin Press. 1996.

Suarez, Gabriel *The Tactical Shotgun The Best Techniques and Tactics for Employing the Shotgun in Personal Combat.* Boulder, CO: Paladin Press. 1996.

Swearengen, Thomas F *The World's Fighting Shotguns Volume IV.* Alexandria VA: T. B. N. Enterprises. 1978.

Sweeting, Sergeant R C *Modern Infantry Weapons and Training in their Use.* Aldershot, UK: Gale & Polden Limited. 1962.

Taylor, Chuck *The Combat Shotgun and Submachine Gun.* Boulder, CO: Paladin Press. 1985

Taylor, Chuck *The Complete Book of Combat Shooting.* Cornville, AZ: Desert Publications. 1982.

Taylor, Major Grant *The Palestine Police Force Close Quarter Battle.* Jerusalem, IS: Government Printer, Palestine. 1972.

Thompson, Leroy *British Commandos in Action.* Carrollton, TX: Squadron Signal Publications Inc. 1987.

Thompson, Leroy *British Paratroops in Action.* Carrollton, TX: Squadron Signal Publications Inc. 1989.

Thompson, Leroy *Dead Clients Don't Pay The Bodyguard's Manual.* Boulder, CO: Paladin Press. 1984.

Thompson, Leroy *De Oppresso Liber The Illustrated History of the U. S. Army Special Forces.* Boulder, CO: Paladin Press. 1987.

Thompson, Leroy *Dirty Wars Elite Forces vs The Guerrillas.* New York, NY: Sterling Publishing Co. 1988.

Thompson, Leroy and Rene Smeets *Great Combat Handguns.* London, UK: Arms and Armor Press. 1993.

Thompson, Leroy and Rene Smeets *Great Combat Handguns A guide to using, collecting and training with handguns.* Poole, UK: Blandford Press. 1987.

Thompson, Leroy *Hostage Rescue Manual.* London, Greenhill Books, 2001; Mechanicsburg, Stackpole Books, 2001.

Thompson, Leroy *Ragged War The Story of Unconventional and Counter-Revolutionary Warfare.* London, UK: Arms and Armor Press 1994.

Thompson, Leroy *The Rescuers The World's Top Anti-Terrorist Units.* Boulder, CO: Paladin Press. 1986.

Thompson, Leroy *SAS Great Britain's Elite Special Air Service.* Osceola, WI: Motorbooks International. 1994.

Thompson, Leroy *United States Airborne Forces 1940–1986.* Poole, UK: Blandford Press 1986.

Thompson, Leroy *US Airborne in Action.* Carrollton, TX: Signal Publications Inc. 1992.

Thompson, Leroy *US Elite Forces – Vietnam.* Carrollton, TX: Signal Publications Inc. 1985.

Thompson, Leroy *US Special Forces 1941–1987.* Poole, UK: Blandford Press 1987.

Tippins, L R *Modern Rifle Shooting in Peace, War and Sport.* London, UK: J. S. Phillips. 1906.

Tracy, Captain C D *The Service Revolver and How to Use It.* London, UK: Harrison and Sons. No date.

Venner, Dominique *Les Armes de la Resistance.* Paris, FR: De L'Imprimerie Herissey. 1976.

Venner, Dominique *Les Armes de Services Speciaux.* Paris, FR: De L'Imprimerie Herissey. 1988.

Walmer, Max *An Illustrated Guide to Modern Elite Forces.* New York, NY: Prentice Hall. 1986.

Westerlin, Dan *Empty Hand, Loaded Gun.* Boulder, CO: Paladin Press. 1984.

Weston, Paul B *Combat Shooting for Police.* Springfield, IL: Charles C. Thomas. 1972.

White, Terry *Fighting Techniques of the Special Forces.* London, UK: Century Random House. 1993.

Williams, Mason *The Law Enforcement Book of Weapons, Ammunition and Training Procedures.* Springfield, IL: Charles C. Thomas. 1977.

Wilson, R K *Textbook of Automatic Pistols.* Prescott, AZ: London, 1900

Winans, Walter *Automatic Pistol Shooting.* London, UK: G P Putnam's Sons. 1915.

Winans, Walter *The Modern Pistol and How to Shoot it.* London, UK: G P Putnam's Sons. 1919.

Winans, Walter *Practical Rifle Shooting.* London, UK: G. P. Putnam's Sons. 1906.

Books and pamphlets with no author

Advanced General Officer Protection. Manchester, MO CQB Training. No date.

Anti-personnel Weapons. London, UK: Taylor & Francis Ltd. 1978.

Combined Operations. New York, NY: MacMillan Company. 1943.

Hostage Rescue Tactics. Manchester, MO. CQB Training. No date.

Infantry Training Volume II The Sub Machine Gun (All Arms). London, UK: Ministry of Defence. 1975.

Machine Guns and Gunnery for Machine Guns. Harrisburg, PA: Telegraph Press. 1954.

The Pistol as a Weapon of Defence. New York, NY: The Industrial Publication Co. 1875.

Authored books and pamphlets with insufficient publication information.

Fairbairn, Captain W E *All-In Fighting.* 1942.

Pollard, Hugh B C *The Pistol in Practice.*

Woodhouse, Arthur Alderson *New Revolver Manual for Police and Infantry Forces.*